Mansfield Turner, William Harris

A Guide to the Institutions and Charities for the Blind in the United Kingdom

Mansfield Turner, William Harris

A Guide to the Institutions and Charities for the Blind in the United Kingdom

ISBN/EAN: 9783337135911

Printed in Europe, USA, Canada, Australia, Japan

Cover: Foto ©ninafisch / pixelio.de

More available books at **www.hansebooks.com**

A GUIDE
TO THE
INSTITUTIONS AND CHARITIES
FOR
THE BLIND

A GUIDE

TO THE

INSTITUTIONS & CHARITIES

FOR

THE BLIND

IN THE UNITED KINGDOM

TO WHICH IS ADDED

INFORMATION RELATING TO THE BLIND AS TO THEIR MANUFACTURES, BOOKS, TYPES, EDUCATION, APPLIANCES, STATISTICAL FIGURES, &c. &c.

BY

MANSFIELD TURNER AND WILLIAM HARRIS

LONDON
SIMPKIN, MARSHALL, & CO.
4 STATIONERS'-HALL COURT
1884

CONTENTS.

	PAGE
PREFACE TO THE PRIVATE EDITION	ix
,, ,, SECOND EDITION	xi
,, ,, FIRST EDITION	xvii
APPENDIX ,, ,, ,, ...	xxiii
STATISTICAL FIGURES FOR 1870 . . .	xxx
,, ,, ,, 1883	xxxi
LIST OF INSTITUTIONS IN UNITED KINGDOM	xxxii
PARTICULARS OF INSTITUTIONS AND WORKSHOPS (Alphabetically arranged)	1–54
LIST OF CHARITIES IN UNITED KINGDOM . . .	55
PARTICULARS OF CHARITIES (Alphabetically arranged) . . .	56–77
HOME TEACHING SOCIETIES	78
LONDON SCHOOL-BOARD CLASSES	80
BOOKS ABOUT THE BLIND	81–90
PUBLISHERS OF BOOKS IN EMBOSSED TYPE . .	90–92
TYPES	92
APPLIANCES	92–95
LIST OF FOREIGN INSTITUTIONS . . .	96, 97
THINGS MADE BY BLIND IN EXHIBITION, 1871	98, 99
ACTS OF PARLIAMENT FOR BLIND . .	100

PREFACE

TO THE

EDITION PRINTED FOR PRIVATE CIRCULATION.

THE following papers are the result of a tour of visits made in the spring of this year, to as many Institutions for the Blind as we knew of, and could conveniently reach, for the purpose of obtaining information which might be of use to our own Institution, then struggling through great difficulties, and also with the hope of inducing some at least of the committees to meet in conference, when a scheme to benefit all Institutions for the Blind might be discussed and matured. During these visits we were struck with the little knowledge each Institution possessed of what was going on elsewhere, and what was being done, or could be done, by blind people; and finding that we were the first persons who had systematically visited these Institutions, and who, therefore, had had an opportunity of comparing them, we determined to print, at our own cost, for private circulation, a short account of each Institution we had visited (it will be observed these comprised the principal ones); and with a view to making a complete book of reference on matters relating to the Blind in the United Kingdom, we invited those Institutions which we had not been able to visit to fill up for us the form we have adopted.

We regret that some of these forms have not been returned to us, and that therefore our work is incomplete; but we hope that when our motives are understood, the value of this work will be more felt, and that these Institutions will assist us to make it complete.

The information here given has in every instance been submitted to the Institution referred to, for revision, and therefore it may be presumed to be correct.

In concluding, we are glad to take this opportunity of expressing our thanks to the committees of those Institutions who received us kindly, and to every one who has rendered us assistance.

We shall always look back with pleasure to some incidents of our tour; and though it has made us feel that much remains to be done to make Institutions for the Blind more useful, and the Blind more independent and happy, we may trust that He who has implanted the desire to benefit the Blind will give strength to fulfil the work, which we feel thankful to know is well begun in the conference so soon to be held at Birmingham.

LEICESTER, *September* 24, 1866.

PREFACE

TO

THE SECOND EDITION.

The exhaustion of the first edition, and the changes that have taken place in the work for the Blind in the thirteen years that have elapsed since that edition was published, induce the authors to revise and republish the 'Guide.' The flattering way in which the first edition was received, leads them to hope that this new edition will be equally acceptable, the more so as they believe that at this particular crisis in the history of the Blind, the information it supplies is greatly needed. As before, the information given of the various Institutions has in every instance been submitted to the managers for correction, and may therefore be relied on as accurate; and though in some few instances the authors have been disappointed in not receiving replies to their inquiries, in these few cases they have taken their information from printed reports issued by those Institutions. They take this opportunity of again thanking all those who have kindly assisted them. The figures in the tabular statements, when compared with those of 1870, show a startling advance in the work for the Blind in every instance.

In 1870, Scotland, with 5 Institutions, sold goods of the value of 21,930*l.*; during the last year reported these 5 Institutions have sold goods amounting to 39,564*l*. England, which in 1870 with 40 Institutions sold only 33,598*l*. worth, during the last year reported has sold more than 73,865*l*. In Ireland, though the returns are too incomplete to give figures, the increase of sales has been very considerable.

In 1870, Scotland on the average benefited 76 Blind in each Institution; during the last year, 98. The total number is 161 in resident Institutions, and 330 in workshops. In 1870 England averaged 43 for each Institution; during the last year, nearly 50. The total number is 1,298 in the Institutions, and 782 in workshops. In Ireland, as far as we can judge, the average now is about the same as in 1870, namely, 60. In 1870 in Scotland the subscriptions, donations, legacies, and income from endowments, amounted to 7,943*l.*—rather more than 20*l.* per head for the number benefited. In the last year reported the amount is 14,021*l.*—nearly 29*l.* per head. In England in 1870 the subscriptions, donations, legacies, and income from endowments, amounted to 31,273*l.*—or about 21*l.* per head for the number benefited; during the last year reported, 56,448*l.*—or about 32*l.* per head. As to Ireland we can make no comparison.

The number of Blind in resident Institutions in England and Scotland has been increased by 410. The number in workshops has been increased (including those attached to resident Institutions) by 254. In England there are nearly 2 in resident Institutions to each 1 in workshops. In Scotland there are 2 in workshops to each 1 in resident Institutions.

Looking at the charities, we find that in England 2,923 persons are receiving pensions, and 392 being benefited in other ways (not including home-teaching societies). The total amount received during the last year, reported by charities, is 35,951*l.*[1]—or 11*l.* per head of those benefited. In Scotland we find no charities distinct from Institutions (other than home-teaching societies). It will thus be seen that out of the 30,000 Blind in the United Kingdom (taking the numbers in Ireland as near as we can judge) there are 2,780 able-bodied Blind being provided for in resident schools and workshops, and 3,393 being assisted by the charities, some few of whom are most likely employed in the workshops. We thus have a total of 6,173, or considerably under one-fourth of the Blind who are being dealt with.

[1] See remarks at money received, page xxxi.

The returns as to embossed type appear to show that Moon's is still used in 35 Institutions; and Braille's, which in 1870 was only in use in 1 Institution, is now used in 27. The other types, it will be seen, are little used.

It ought to be noticed as a sign of the great advance in the interest felt for the work in aid of the Blind, that since 1870 there have been called together to consider the affairs of the Blind:—

1. A Special Committee of the Charity Organisation Society in 1876, which after forty meetings published a most useful report on the subject.

2. A Conference held by the School Board of London on the instruction of the Blind children in 1878. Report published.

3. A Conference at York, largely and influentially attended, in 1883. Report published.

4. And within the last two months a meeting has been held at Grosvenor House, invited by the Duke of Westminster, to discuss the question of an application for a Royal Commission to consider the condition of the Blind.

Again, the number of home-teaching societies has increased so largely since 1870, that we now only give a list of them lest we should inconveniently increase the size of our book, and for the same reason we now dispense with the list of books published in embossed types. Since 1870 the interest shown in the work for the Blind has also been manifested by some very large legacies left to aid in the furtherance of the work.

The advance in the last few years, it will be seen, has been great and hopeful. Let us now look for a moment to the future. As the importance of retail shops, for the sale of goods made by the Blind, has been fully shown by the increase of sales, we may hope that they will further increase and improve, and that still greater efforts will be made in this direction. As one means of overcoming a great difficulty, viz., the disposal of the goods made by the Blind, which, at present, seems to be considered insuperable, we ventured, in the first edition of the 'Guide,' to suggest a remedy, the principle of which has been fully confirmed by the Committee of the Charity Organisation Society, and by the Conference at York, viz., the establishment of a Central Association for the benefit of all Institutions for the Blind (the idea is explained in the Preface to first edition); and as the influence of the Gardner Trustees seems now to be directed to the furtherance of such a scheme, we have hope that it will ere long be carried out. To further such a scheme will, we trust, be the aim of all Institutions for the Blind, which should be united as one great co-operative society, if they are to be prosperous. We would also draw attention to the large number of sighted teachers and helpers now employed, as compared with a few years ago, believing that their employment must tend to improvement in the quality of the work made by the Blind. It will be noticed that in one or two cases those sighted helpers are deaf and dumb; the subject of the employment of this class was brought forward at the York Conference, and we hope will receive increased attention, as it must be manifest that if, in helping the Blind, we can also help this other afflicted class, we shall largely increase the usefulness of our work, and the amount of public sympathy given to it. And this idea will, we think, if it can be carried out, help to solve a great difficulty in the work for the Blind, viz., the comparatively small results achieved, in return for the very great exertions and large amount of money expended upon it; and we commend to the thoughtful the question whether 110,700*l.* in one year, with the labour paid and unpaid, given to its use, ought not to produce greater results than at present?

In conclusion, we trust it will not be forgotten that if all our efforts to provide employment and independence for the ablebodied Blind, are successful, there will remain at least 10,000 sick and infirm Blind who demand our help and sympathy. Pensions are now almost the only mode of help given to them, and they too often, we fear, benefit the sighted relatives and the poor's rates more than the Blind; at any rate, there are no sufficient means to provide all with pensions. It is true that home-teaching societies are able, through private sources, to alleviate some of the most distressing cases, but there is a large number, especially in the towns, who lead very wretched lives, and to make these lives more tolerable is an object worthy of the highest philanthropy; and surely there are other and better ways than pensions, by which these suffering ones might be assisted. We look forward with hope to a day when the successfully employed labour of the able-bodied Blind will be able to yield such a return as may partially help to supply means to alleviate the misery of many of the infirm and feeble ones. If we could only see the committees of the various Institutions actuated by a desire to make a strong pull all together, instead of being satisfied with isolation, the future would have a bright prospect, for there are workers enough! there are large funds! and 'a good time' might be confidently expected, when all the able-bodied Blind, aided by the sighted to help themselves, should be satisfied that their own labour will suffice to supply them with a living, and when every sick and suffering Blind one shall be an object of careful thought.

We put forth this second edition of the 'Guide,' in the hope of forwarding this object, asking the friends of the Blind to accept our effort, and to be lenient in criticising any errors or imperfections which may have escaped our notice, and asking also for the Divine blessing upon this, our labour of love.

LEICESTER, *August*, 1884.

PREFACE

TO

THE FIRST EDITION.

In offering to the public this 'Guide,' which in 1866 was printed for private circulation only, we think it right to state some of the reasons why we have published it; and to offer some remarks on the subject-matter of the book. Among other reasons are the number of letters we received, requesting copies of the unpublished 'Guide,' and asking for information about the Blind, coupled with the great difficulty we ourselves often experienced in getting information on the subject when we needed it. The fact that the condition of the Blind occupies at the present time a large share of public interest is evidenced by the attention of the House of Commons having been lately drawn to their condition; by their having been lately the subject of correspondence in the London newspapers; by the fact that the Institutions for the Blind were invited by Her Majesty's Commissioners to send articles made by, and relating to, the Blind to the International Exhibition this year; and lastly, that of late years so many Institutions and Charities have been established for their benefit.[1]

[1] In the year 1800 there were only four Institutions for the Blind in the Kingdom; during the next thirty years six others were added to the list; in the succeeding thirty years seventeen more were opened; while within the last ten years twenty new ones have been established, making a total now of fifty-three, without including Societies for Visiting the Blind at their homes, and other Charities.

In almost every instance the information inserted in the 'Guide' has been collected by personal inquiry, and from printed reports and papers; and been submitted to the Secretary of each Society for correction, if needed. In some instances we have not received any reply to our communication; we therefore presume that the statement submitted was correct.

The figures in the tabular statement annexed are drawn from the 'Guide,' and show some curious facts. Scotland, with five Institutions, sold, in the last year of which we have any report, goods of the value of 21,930*l.*; while England, with forty Institutions, only sold in the same period goods of the value of 33,598*l.*; and Ireland only 454*l.*

Scotland provides for (on an average) seventy-six Blind in each Institution, while England only provides for forty-three, and Ireland for sixty.

The donations and subscriptions in Scotland for the same year amount to more than 20*l.* per head of the number benefited, while in England they only amount to about 21*l.*, and in Ireland to about 16*l.*

So far as returns have reached us, it appears that Mr. Moon's system of reading for the Blind is adopted by thirty-eight Institutions and Home-teaching Societies; while only twenty-one use the books of other systems.[1]

Of the 30,000 Blind in the Kingdom, there are only about 2,250 being instructed or assisted to work. The total amount received per annum for the Blind, according to the answers received, is about 66,000*l.*; but this only represents the amount reported in this 'Guide:' besides this, there are twelve Societies from which we have no return.

Of Institutions for the Blind generally we may remark that in our search for information we have been struck with the fact that at each Institution nearly the same difficulties appear to exist, the principal one being the difficulty of selling the goods manu-

---

[1] Moon's, thirty-eight. Lucas's, seven. Roman, four. Alston's, four. Frere's, three. Braille, four.

factured at such prices as will secure a ready sale, and cover the cost of production; and consequently, in most instances, there is a large surplus stock. In cases where the stock is wholly disposed of, our observations lead us to think that sales have been secured by selling at a loss.

It is most important that the origin of this difficulty should be discovered and, if possible, removed. We will, therefore, now point out what appears to us to be some of the causes of it, and venture to suggest a remedy.

First, it appears that it is too generally assumed that the labour of the Blind *cannot* be remunerative, and therefore the business part of the Institutions is often conducted without energy, and the ordinary principles of business are ignored: for instance, it has too often happened that when an Institution has been formed, unsuitable premises, in a back street, have been selected, and a blind man engaged as a teacher or shopkeeper; or at best, a sighted man has been appointed to overlook two or more trades, being unacquainted with at least one of them. Again, it has too often been the rule in the shop, that nothing should be sold which was not made by the Blind, so that (as there are many articles of daily use which the Blind cannot make) the shop has been unable to supply all goods of the class in which it professed to deal. Again, in purchasing material, &c., how often the manager when first appointed knows little or nothing of the qualities, &c., of some of the material and stock required, and is therefore obliged to trust to the principle of the seller! Lastly, in the manufacture of goods, instead of being able to concentrate the labours of the Blind upon the production of articles belonging to one branch of trade, as in the case of the sighted (by which cheapness and quickness might be attained), the workers are, through the necessities of over-stock, obliged to be 'Jacks of all trades,' to the detriment of the manufacture; to the loss of the Blind, who generally cannot attain proficiency or quickness; and to the idea on the part of the public that blind-made articles are dear and of bad quality. This is not the way an ordinary business is conducted, and it is not surprising that in the case of the Blind it should not be successful.

Let us now suggest how we think this great difficulty may be met; and if our plan does not commend itself to all as the best remedy, our purpose will be answered if it sets men thinking on the subject.

We start with the proved fact that the Blind, assisted by the sighted, can produce certain articles quite equal in quality to those made by the sighted. At Bradford in Yorkshire, the Committee remark that 'the Institution competes successfully with other manufacturers as regards quality,' and the fact that in one year the Institution sold goods of the value of nearly 5,000*l*. proves the assertion. In Scotland, also, the amount of goods sold proves that goods made by the Blind can compete with any in point of quality.

How can these goods be produced without loss? First, we believe this may be done by employing much more sighted labour in conjunction with that of the Blind. The blind man can perform certain parts of the work as quickly and well as the sighted; let *him* perform *that* part only. Secondly, we should advise that the sale of goods made by the Blind should be largely extended by means of retail shops in very large towns. (To begin with, let every Institution have a first-rate shop in a first-rate situation, and be assured that, if well managed, it will yield an annual income to its funds, after all expenses are paid.) Thirdly, we advise that an Association for the purposes of trade be formed by all Institutions manufacturing and trading in goods made by the Blind; by this means the trade throughout the country would be brought under one system, with one common interest, and each Institution should be as far as possible enabled to confine its attention to one branch of trade.

Finally, we advise that Schools for the Blind should only be places of *instruction* in mental and industrial training; that blind pupils should be taught one trade only, as are the sighted; and that all trades be carried on in manufactories (workshops) where sighted and blind persons work together. We believe the results of this scheme would be that all the able-bodied Blind could be provided with constant employment, thereby rendering them, as a class, independent, and affording great relief to the ratepayers of this country.

We trust our 'Guide' will be found useful to those who take an interest in the Blind. It will at least demonstrate that an increasing interest and care is taken in the temporal and eternal welfare of the Blind.

Our thanks are due to those who have assisted us in the preparation of the 'Guide;' we trust they will feel that the object we have in view was worthy of their help, however imperfectly we have carried it out.

We conclude with thanks to God, who has permitted us to undertake and complete this book; and with prayers for His blessing upon it we send it forth.

LEICESTER, *July*, 1871.

The difficulty spoken of on pages xviii and xix exists in other countries besides our own, and since writing the above preface we have ascertained one instance in which it has been overcome. In confirmation of our views as to the remedy, we draw attention to extracts from the Twentieth (1866) and Twenty-fourth (1870) Reports of the Indiana (U.S.) Institution for the Blind. *Vide* Appendix.[1]

[1] This appendix is given in this second edition, next page.

APPENDIX

TO

THE FIRST EDITION.

Extracts from the 20th and 24th Annual Reports of the Trustees and Superintendent of the Indiana Institute for the Education of the Blind.—By W. H. CHURCHMAN, Esq., A.M., Superintendent.

On page 24 of the 20th Report (for the year 1866), under 'Work Department,' the Superintendent says—'Under the efficient management of the present contractor, Mr. J. W. Bradshaw, who has been in charge of the shops since April 1 last, they have been carried on with more system, and with better results to the pupils, in the matter of their instruction, than ever before since the foundation of the Institution. He conducts them as an individual enterprise, upon the plan introduced some five years since, and we are more than ever convinced of the correctness of the system in its application to shops of this kind. The Institution is free from the trouble and expense of providing the raw materials and the necessary instructors, as well as from the care, sale, and delivery of the manufactured articles, together with the risk of accumulation and depreciation in prices when the market is dull; while the pupils are more thoroughly trained in skill, industry, and the economical use of materials than they are likely to be under the old system of salaried instructors. Whatever is to the advantage of the contractor, is likewise to the advantage of the pupil under instruction. If the self-interest of the former impels him to require of the latter that he shall be promptly in his place at the proper time; that he shall work industriously, rapidly, and skilfully while there; and that he shall, in all cases, use his materials to the best advantage, without unnecessary waste, surely the learner is thereby made so much the better mechanic, and hence, put into the best possible condition for obtaining employment after the completion of his trade.

'Ours is, we believe, the only Institution of the kind where this system prevails, and we should abandon it with extreme reluctance, after our more than five years' experience.

'It is objected by some with whom we have conversed upon the subject, that, under our plan, the instructor must be liable to neglect the dull of learning, and give his special attention to the more expert. But we have never found any difficulty upon this head so far, and certainly believe that there is no more to be apprehended than under the ordinary system. Moreover, this is strictly provided against in our contract with the conductor of the shops. The superintendent relinquishes nothing of his former control in such matters.

'It is also objected that the contractor cannot sustain himself under such an arrangement, inasmuch as no Institution has been able to do so without a more or less pecuniary loss; but our contractor has done it for years, and thus the objection is effectually set aside. Were he to confine himself to the labour of the pupils alone, much of whose work is necessarily inferior, as that of young apprentices, the plan might be less successful. But such is not the case. We permit him to employ, in connection with the pupils, as many skilful journeymen, either blind or seeing, as his business will warrant, and find that the learners, as well as himself, are the gainers thereby in several respects. They are stimulated by the example of the finished workmen to work better and faster, and their general character is favourably influenced by intimate association with experienced seeing persons from the outer world, a circumstance which should have considerable weight with the intelligent educator of the Blind.

'For the contractor, the employment of additional workmen possesses several advantages. It enables him to extend his business, and give it the character of other establishments where the same kind of work is manufactured; also, to work off the inferior products of his inexperienced apprentices, in connection with the better ware manufactured by the finished workmen; and when the number of pupils in the shops is too limited to enable him to supply the demand created by a judicious management of his business, as is the case at present with us, it enables him to retain his customers, by obviating the necessity of their going elsewhere for the time being, at the risk of losing them altogether. For example, we have, at this time, no pupils who are desirous of learning the carpet-weaving business; yet there is a brisk demand in the market for this article, which must be supplied, or the trade is lost to the Institution. Hence the looms are kept at work by seeing *employés* for the time being, until some pupils are received who wish to learn the business.

It need hardly be remarked that the contractor is in no case permitted to occupy the shops with seeing workmen, to the exclusion or detriment of our pupils.'

Near the bottom of page 65 of the same Report Mr. Churchman says, in speaking of the 'results' of instruction given in Schools for the Blind :—

'The masses have left school, after passing through a nominal course of instruction, greatly improved in many respects, it were useless to deny, but, nevertheless, without that thorough practical development of character which is necessary to put them in a condition for successful competition with others in " the battle of life."

'This may be an inevitable result, but after thirty years of practical experience with the obstacles, real and imaginary, which are strewn along the pathway of the sightless, all of which years, with slight exceptions, have been spent in connection with Institutions for the Blind, we cannot so regard it. Nor can we withhold an expression of our honest convictions upon the subject. Give to your blind children, in reality, as well as in profession, an equal opportunity with your seeing ones, for thoroughness of physical and mental training, and we are sure you will receive a more satisfactory return for your investment of time and money in establishments for their education.

'But in what direction must we look, you will naturally ask, for the causes of the disappointment adverted to? In answer to this inquiry, it may be affirmed, with due deference to the *motives* of our colabourers in the interesting field which engages our mutual attention, that the true bearings of the subject have not been thoroughly apprehended, and, as a consequence, the real difficulties of the case have been but imperfectly provided for.

'Judging from the prevailing practice of Institutions, it has been virtually assumed by their founders and managers, that to take a blind child from his home among cruelly indulgent friends, with unawakened mental faculties and undeveloped physical powers, and place him, with these unfavourable antecedents, in an Institution for a period of five, six, or seven years, is to put him upon an equal footing with his seeing brother. In this brief time, the former is expected to acquire a thorough English education, commencing with his A, B, C, and become a skilful performer and teacher of music, or perfect himself in one or more mechanical arts. While the latter, with the advantages of a very different sort of home training, excellent schools of every grade, and well-appointed workshops or other places of business, is allowed all the years of his minority to prepare himself for the duties and trials of life.

'This assumption is palpably absurd. It might be less so, however, were our Institutions provided with facilities, in the way of apparatus,

&c., equal to those of the best educational establishments for the seeing, which, unfortunately, is not the case. Most of these things have to be constructed especially for the blind student; and the demand for them is so small that, in the absence of the usual stimulus of competition in their production, they are quite expensive. Therefore, as their importance is not duly appreciated by those who furnish the pecuniary means, we are, as a general thing, but scantily provided with them. Moreover, such appliances as we have are mostly of rude construction, and but poorly adapted to the end in view.

'Again, as a consequence, perhaps, of the limited term for which pupils are usually received into our Institutions, or, it may be, from lack of correct views as to the most effective methods of teaching, the minds of the pupils are distracted by imposing upon them a multiplicity of studies and occupations at the same time. Their ordinary school branches; their vocal and instrumental music; their mechanical employments, sometimes two or three of these, must, it is thought, be carried on simultaneously. Otherwise, their term of instruction will have expired ere they can make a passable show of having accomplished their object in coming to school. And as to systematic physical culture, this generally receives little or no attention. Indeed, there is no time for it, consistently with the crowding system pursued; nor is its necessity appreciated.

'It seems never to have occurred to the managers of our Institutions for the Blind, that, in requiring their pupils to master a trade, or other profession, to be used as a means of gaining a livelihood, simultaneously with the acquirement of their school education, they are asking more of them than is expected of seeing youths, with their superior advantages. True, manual labour schools for the seeing have been tried in a few instances, but they have, in each case, been abandoned as unsuccessful experiments. It has been found that their graduates make neither good scholars nor good mechanics, much less both. Why, then, pursue this exploded system with the Blind?'

Then on page 68 of the same Report:—

'Moreover, in the departments of music and handicraft, the only ones depended upon for preparing the pupils for self-maintenance, there is not usually that efficiency of drill which may be found in establishments for the seeing. Nor can it be otherwise, while the crowding system above alluded to continues to be pursued. Besides, the plan upon which the business of the workshops is generally conducted does not comport with the principle which we are striving to advocate in this communication. Were the parties in charge of them personally interested in the results, as is the case with ordinary manufacturing establishments, the apprentices would be better trained in all respects, and hence, better prepared to make their way in the world after finishing their course of instruction. But as this subject is elsewhere treated upon at some length, we forbear further comments here.

'Still further, the general policy of our Institutions, with regard to the employment of teachers, has not been such as to insure the best possible results to their pupils. It has been a "penny wise and pound foolish" policy. Unlike schools for the deaf and dumb, we have not, as a rule, offered sufficient inducements in the way of salary for persons of the right kind of qualifications to prepare themselves for our peculiar work, and continue in it as a life-long business.

'The burthen of our teaching having thus far been of an elementary character, it has apparently been thought that any one of moderate qualifications for teaching in seeing schools should be competent to teach the Blind. Whereas, a proper examination into the subject will show that the rudimentary instruction and training of minds which suffer from the closing up of one of the principal avenues of knowledge, require even higher qualifications in the teacher, than the branches which are subsequently taught, after the faculties have been brought into a condition of full activity. It is gratifying to know, however, that there are, of late years, some indications of improvement in this direction.

'Finally, the result of all these things is, that our graduates launch their frail barks upon the ocean of life in a condition but ill calculated to weather the storms they must needs encounter; and when they founder, as founder they must, a cry of necessary incompetency salutes their ears. But whose fault is it? Surely not theirs. Did they possess, instead of mere smatterings of knowledge upon a few subjects, accompanied with fourth-rate skill in performing upon some musical instrument, or in plying some half-learned manual art, a thorough, harmonious development of the mental and physical powers, such as results from the training received by seeing persons, the case would be far different. . . . . By some of our co-labourers we may be charged with censoriousness, in giving expression thus frankly to our honest convictions. If any such there are, we would assure them that we are actuated by no other motive than an earnest desire to promote the well-being of a class, for the amelioration of whose unfortunate condition we have thus far spent the best years of our life.'—Indianapolis. *November* 1, 1866.

In the Report of last year (1870), after four more years' experience, Mr. Churchman remarks, on page 23 :—

'The usual system of conducting the industrial department of establishments like ours, is to employ salaried instructors and other assistants, who are entrusted, under the general direction of the superintendent, with the purchase of materials and sale of manufactured articles, all of which is done without any pecuniary risk or responsibility on the part of such *employés*. Under this system the workshops are seldom, or never, self sustaining, if the salaries are reckoned with the expenses. On the contrary, they are often a source of considerable expense. The reasons for this are mainly as follows:—1. The shops being designed as places of instruction merely, the workmen are mostly unskilled apprentices, and therefore turn out much work which is unsaleable or must be disposed of at a price which does not yield a profit. 2. The purchases and sales are not made as judiciously by salaried *employés*, as by persons who are doing business on their own account; and 3. Such *employés* are not as careful to exact of their operatives the same quality and quantity of work, and the same economy in the use of materials, as those who are interested in the financial results of the shops under their charge.

'Following in the footsteps of the then existing Institutions, our shops were commenced in 1847, under the prevailing system of management, and so continued during the first fourteen years after the opening of the Institute. But in 1861, it being thought that greater efficiency and economy might be secured by a change of plan, it was resolved to try our present system, which we have continued from that time without interruption. During an experience of over nine years, we have become more and more convinced of the correctness of the principle involved, and could not be induced to return voluntarily to our original plan of management. The principle adverted to, is that of pecuniary interest and responsibility on the part of the conductor of the shops. We furnish him the building and the tools, without nominal rent, and he has the pupils instructed in their trades at his own cost, as a compensation therefor. All purchases, sales, and other business transactions connected with the shops, are made by him on his own account, and he is therefore the sole gainer or loser by the result. All the direct interest we have in the matter is, that the shops be conducted in harmony with the general regulations of the Institution, and the pupils faithfully instructed in the trades assigned them by the Superintendent. These objects are secured by a rigid contract and bond.

'As the labour of the apprentices alone cannot be made sufficiently productive to meet the necessary expenses of the department, or supply the demand for manufactured articles created by an efficient management of its concerns, the contractor is allowed to employ skilled workmen, either blind or seeing, as journeymen, to supplement the unskilled labour of the pupils. In no other way can the conduct of such an establishment be made to afford sufficient inducement to any man of proper business qualifications to engage in it as a personal enterprise. And while this feature of our system enables us to procure the instruction of our pupils without cost to the Institution, it incidentally offers a valuable stimulus to them, by bringing them into association with skilful and dexterous workmen as exemplars.

'As illustrating the greater economy of the present over the former system, your attention is asked to the following statement:—

'During the seven years preceding its adoption, the expenses of the work department were, according to the published reports of the trustees, in excess of the receipts to the amount of $6,206. 63, showing an average loss of $886. 66 per annum, and that without reckoning the salaries of the instructors.

'Now, if we multiply this average annual deficit by nine, making $7,979. 94, and add to the product the sum of $5,400 as the salary of a competent instructor and manager for nine years at $600, the lowest rate of compensation for which the services of such an officer could have been secured, we will have $13,379. 94 as a fair estimate of what it would have cost the Institution to carry on the shops under the old system during the past nine years. Whereas, under the present system, the actual outlay for the same period has been only $519. 66 for tools and fixtures, most, if not all, of which are still on hand and worth their cost. Surely this saving of $13,000, to say nothing of the superiority of the present plan of management in other respects, is worthy of serious consideration.

'In the above comparative statement, it is hardly necessary to say, no account has been made of the costs of keeping the shops in repair, or of fuel for warming them under either system.

'It may not be amiss to state before leaving this subject that an examination of the reports of other Institutions, whose industrial departments are conducted upon the plan first explained, will show equally unfavourable results.'

1870.

Number of Blind provided for by Institutions	Resident Schools	Workshops	Outworkers at Resident Schools	Total	Charities: Money Charities	Charities: Home Teaching Societies, &c.	Remarks
England	932	484	107	1,523	2,108	1,840	5 Workshops have made no returns. The average would be about 15 at each, not included in the total given
Scotland	117	15	252	384	Nil	935	—
Ireland	300	Nil	Nil	300	87	Nil	—

	Sales during last year given	Subscriptions and Donations for last year	Endowment (per annum)	Income of Charities, Sub. & Don.	Charities Endowment (per annum)	Highest and lowest charged at Institutions	Remarks
England	33,528	£25,196	£6,077 For 14 Institutions	5,318	15,042	£ s. 25 10 / 5 4 And Income Nil	3 Institutions make no returns of sales, say £500 per annum each; 5 Institutions make no return of Subscriptions, say £1,500. These are not included in the total given
Scotland	21,930	6,588	1,355	1,216	5	15 0 / 10 0	1 Institution, which is not included, makes no returns of sales. In 1865 its sales were £3,112
Ireland	454	3,588	1,220	312	Considerable but no returns	18 0 / 1 13	2 Institutions have not sent any return. We have given the average of one of them for 3 years, and included it in the total

System of Reading	Moon	Roman	Frere	Alston	Lucas	Braille	Remarks
England	29 Institutions or Societies	5 Institutions or Societies	3 Institutions or Societies	1 Institution or Society	7 Institutions or Societies	1 Institution or Society	4 made no return
Scotland	7 ditto	—	—	2 ditto	—	1 ditto	—
Ireland	2 ditto	—	—	1 ditto	1	—	2 make no return

xxxi

Country	No. of Blind taught and employed			No. of Blind beneficed by Charities		Teachers employed			Goods not made by the Blind at which sold	Remarks
	In Resident Institutions	In Workshops	In Workshops attached to Resident Institutions	Total taught and employed	By pensions	By other means	Blind	Sighted	Both	Institutions at which sold	
England	1,298	528	254	2,080	2,923	392	9	24	7	25	1 Workshop gives no return.
Scotland	161	54	276	491	—	6	—	5	—	4	2 Charities, ditto.
Ireland	166	43	Nil	209	—	27	1	2	1	1	1 Institution gives no return. 1 Institution gives no return of numbers.

Money Received

Country	By Institutions and Workshops				By Charities			Remarks
	Sales during last year reported	Subscriptions, Donations, Legacies, last year reported	Endowment per annum	Total per Annum, without Sales	Subscriptions, Donations, Legacies for last year reported	Endowment		
	£	£	£	£	£	£		Since these figures have been in type, it has been found that an English Charity with an income of £4,050l. per ann. was not included in the returns; the amount of monies received by charities is incorrect to that extent.
England	72,865	52,606	13,842	66,448	6,856	29,095		2 Institutions give no return on these subjects.
Scotland	39,564	12,419	1,602	14,021	—	—		
Ireland	4,682	4,163	1,836	5,999	787	107		2 Institutions give no returns.

Types for the Blind.

Country	Number of Institutions using					Remarks
	Moon	Roman	Frere	Alston	Lucas	Braille	
England	26	5	—	—	5	21	7 Workshops give no returns.
Scotland	4	—	1	1	4	4	
Ireland	5	1	—	1	—	2	

ENGLAND has 21 Resident Schools (without Worcester College), and 8 Schools have Workshops attached; SCOTLAND has 4 Resident Schools, all of which have workshops attached; IRELAND has 3 Resident Schools.
Resident Institutions in England closed since 1870.— London, Alexandra, Worcester.
Workshops in England closed since 1870.— Hastings, Ipswich, London, Spitalfields.
Resident Schools opened in England since 1870.—London, Kilburn; London Royal Normal College; Sheffield; Wolverhampton.
Workshops opened in England since 1874.— Bristol and Clifton; Carlisle; London, Greenwich, Kensington; Sunderland.
In Scotland a Workshop has been opened at Inverness since 1870.

List of Institutions for the Blind in the United Kingdom.

RESIDENT INSTITUTIONS.

ENGLAND.

	PAGE
Bath (Walcot Parade)	3
Bath (Bathwick Street)	4
Birmingham [1]	7
Brighton	9
Bristol	10
Devonport	17
Exeter [1]	22
Leeds [1]	27
Liverpool (Hardman Street)	29
Liverpool (Brunswick Road)	31
London (St. George's) [1]	32
London (St. John's Wood)	33
London (Upper Norwood)	35
London (Kilburn)	37
Manchester [1]	39
Newcastle-on-Tyne (Northumberland Street)	40
Norwich	42
Nottingham [1]	43
Plymouth [1]	46
Sheffield [1]	47
Southsea [1]	48
Swansea	51
Wolverhampton	52
Worcester College	53
York	54

SCOTLAND.

	PAGE
Aberdeen [1]	1
Edinburgh [1]	21
Glasgow [1]	23
Inverness [1]	26

IRELAND.

	PAGE
Armagh	2
Belfast (Ulster Society)	5
Cork	16
Dublin (Molyneux)	19
Dublin (Richmond)	18

[1] Workshops attached for outdoor journeymen.

WORKSHOPS.

ENGLAND.

	PAGE
Bradford	8
Bristol and Clifton	11
Bolton	12
Cardiff	13
Carlisle	14
Cheltenham	15
Greenwich	24
Hull	25
Leicester	28
Liverpool (Cornwallis Street)	30
London (Berners Street)	34
London (Kensington)	36
Manchester	38
Newcastle-on-Tyne (Blackett Street)	41
Peckham	44
Preston	45
Stockport	49
Sunderland	50

SCOTLAND.

	PAGE
Dundee	20

IRELAND.

	PAGE
Belfast (Royal Avenue)	6

ABERDEEN.

ASYLUM FOR THE BLIND,
HUNTLY STREET, ABERDEEN.

Secretaries . . . . { Mr. DAVIDSON,
{ Mr. GARDEN.

1. Number of Blind in the Town?
2. Objects of the Institution; if school, nature of Education?—
In a resident school to provide instruction in reading and ordinary branches of education for Blind children, to teach trades, and to provide workshops.
3. When founded?—1812.
4. What system of Reading in use?—Moon and Braille.
5. What number of male and female inmates, and amount charged (if any) for each?—Males, 12. 10*l.* per annum.
6. Age of admission, and how long they may remain?—6 to 16.
7. Qualification of Candidates for Admission?—Preference given to those who have been born or resided for 3 years in the Counties of Aberdeen, Banff, and Kincardine; the Candidate must be indigent, healthy, and of good character.
8. What Industrial occupations and trades are carried on—by males: and by females?—Basket making, mat making, matting, netting, twine, and mattresses.
9. Are outdoor pupils received for instruction in trades, and up to what age?—Yes.
10. How many Blind employed in the workshops?—58.
11. Blind or sighted teachers? Are sighted workmen employed to assist in finishing blind work, or as journeymen?— Sighted teachers.
12. Is there a retail shop?—Yes: at the Institution.
13. If so, are goods not made by the Blind sold in it?—Yes.
14. What amount of goods were sold from the warehouse and retail shop last year, 1883?—5,131.
15. When do the Managing Committee meet?—Quarterly.
16. What were the subscriptions last year, 1883?— } 203*l.*
17. What were donations and legacies last year, 1883?— }
18. What income from endowments or trust funds?—365*l.*
19. General remarks.—

ARMAGH.

MACAN ASYLUM FOR THE BLIND,
ARMAGH.

Secretary . . T. SMITH, Esq.

1. Number of Blind in the Town?
2. Objects of the Institution; if school, nature of Education?—The support of Blind people, principally from the County of Armagh.
3. When founded?—1854.
4. What system of Reading in use?—Moon and Roman.
5. What number of male and female inmates, and amount charged (if any) for each?—16 males.
6. Age of admission, and how long they may remain?—No limit of age; remain during good behaviour.
7. Qualification of Candidates for Admission?—Poverty.
8. What Industrial occupations and trades are carried on—by males: and by females?—Basket making.
9. Are outdoor pupils received for instruction in trades, and up to what age?
10. How many Blind employed in the workshops?—10; the rest are old men.
11. Blind or sighted teachers? Are sighted workmen employed to assist in finishing blind work, or as journeymen?—Blind. No.
12. Is there a retail shop?—No.
13. If so, are goods not made by the Blind sold in it?
14. What amount of goods were sold from the warehouse and retail shop last year, 1883?
51. When do the Managing Committee meet?—Monthly.
16. What were the subscriptions last year, 1883?
17. What were donations and legacies last year, 1883?
18. What income from endowments or trust funds?
19. General remarks.—The Asylum is entirely supported by the endowment of the late Mr. A. J. Macan, of Armagh.

BATH.

INSTITUTION FOR THE BLIND AND DEAF AND DUMB,

8 & 9 WALCOT PARADE, BATH.

Honorary Secretary . . Miss ELWIN.

1. Number of Blind in the Town?
2. Objects of the Institution; if school, nature of Education?—In a resident school to provide instruction for Blind and Deaf and Dumb children, of a religious and elementary character.
3. When founded?—1850.
4. What system of Reading in use?—Moon's chiefly.
5. What number of male and female inmates, and amount charged (if any) for each?—30. 17 blind. 12*l.* per annum.
6. Age of admission, and how long they may remain?—Females, 6 to 16 years. Males, 6 to 14 years.
7. Qualification of Candidates for Admission?—Health and capacity to receive instruction.
8. What Industrial occupations and trades are carried on—by males: and by females?—Basket work.
9. Are outdoor pupils received for instruction in trades, and up to what age?—No.
10. How many Blind employed in the workshops?
11. Blind or sighted teachers? Are sighted workmen employed to assist in finishing blind work, or as journeymen?—Sighted teachers.
12. Is there a retail shop?—Yes: at the Institution.
13. If so, are goods not made by the Blind sold in it?
14. What amount of goods were sold from the warehouse and retail shop last year, 1883?—20*l.*
15. When do the Managing Committee meet?—Monthly.
16. What were the subscriptions last year, 1883?—139*l.*
17. What were donations and legacies last year, 1883?—67*l.*
18. What income from endowments or trust funds?
19. General remarks.—

BATH.

BLIND SCHOOL HOME,

36 BATHWICK STREET, BATH.

Honorary Secretary . . Miss LOUISA BROKE.

1. Number of Blind in the Town?
2. Objects of the Institution; if school, nature of Education?—To support 12 Blind women previously educated at Miss Elwin's Institution for Blind and Deaf and Dumb Children, at 9 Walcot Parade, Bath.
3. When founded?—1857.
4. What system of Reading in use?—Lucas, Moon, Braille.
5. What number of male and female inmates, and amount charged (if any) for each?—12 females. 12*l.* a year.
6. Age of admission, and how long they may remain?—17 years or over; remain while paid for and of good behaviour.
7. Qualification of Candidates for Admission?—Good character from Institute and skill in basket making.
8. What Industrial occupations and trades are carried on—by males: and by females?—Caning chairs, knitting, and fine basket work.
9. Are outdoor pupils received for instruction in trades, and up to what age?—No.
10. How many Blind employed in the workshops?—None.
11. Blind or sighted teachers? Are sighted workmen employed to assist in finishing blind work, or as journeymen?—Sighted teachers.
12. Is there a retail shop?—Yes: at the Institution.
13. If so, are goods not made by the Blind sold in it?
14. What amount of goods were sold from the warehouse and retail shop last year, 1883?—After paying cost of teaching and materials, 15*l.* was cleared.
15. When do the Managing Committee meet?—When needful.
16. What were the subscriptions last year, 1883?—111*l.*
17. What were donations and legacies last year, 1883?—149*l.*
18. What income from endowments or trust funds?
19. General remarks.—

BELFAST.

THE ULSTER SOCIETY FOR PROMOTING THE EDUCATION OF THE DEAF AND DUMB AND THE BLIND, BELFAST.

Honorary Secretaries . . { Sir CHAS. LANYON, CHAS. W. SHAW, Esq.

1. Number of Blind in the Town?—About 180.
2. Objects of the Institution; if school, nature of Education? In a resident school to instruct the Blind and Deaf and Dumb in the ordinary branches of knowledge, with a religious education in accordance with the doctrinal standards of the Churches of England and Scotland. Also to teach trades.
3. When founded?—1831.
4. What system of Reading in use?—Alston, Moon, Braille.
5. What number of male and female inmates, and amount charged (if any) for each?—Deaf and Dumb, 79; Blind, 24.
6. Age of admission, and how long they may remain?—8 to 13, except special cases, and remain till fairly educated.
7. Qualification of Candidates for Admission?—Residence in Ulster for free admission; sometimes paying pupils are received from beyond this limit.
8. What Industrial occupations and trades are carried on—by males: and by females?—Blind pupils. Males taught mat making, girls knitting and some house work where capable. Some blind born, instrumental music.
9. Are outdoor pupils received for instruction in trades, and up to what age?
10. How many Blind employed in the workshops?—All who are capable of any work.
11. Blind or sighted teachers? Are sighted workmen employed to assist in finishing blind work, or as journeymen?—Sighted. No.
12. Is there a retail shop?—Yes.
13. If so, are goods not made by the Blind sold in it?—No.
14. What amount of goods were sold from the warehouse and retail shop last year, 1883?
15. When do the Managing Committee meet?—Monthly.
16. What were the subscriptions last year, 1883?
17. What were the donations and legacies last year, 1883?—2,131*l*.
18. What income from endowments or trust funds?—About 800*l*.
19. General remarks.—

BELFAST.

WORKSHOPS FOR INDUSTRIOUS BLIND,
ROYAL AVENUE, BELFAST.

Honorary Secretaries . { L. M. EWART, Esq.
{ A. D. LEMON, Esq.

1. Number of Blind in the Town?—Between 200 and 300.
2. Objects of the Institution; if school, nature of Education?— To teach trades and to give employment to the Blind.
3. When founded?—1871.
4. What system of Reading in use?—Moon.
5. What number of male and female inmates, and amount charged (if any) for each?
6. Age of admission, and how long they may remain?—14 to 40. Remain till unable to work.
7. Qualification of Candidates for Admission?—Blindness.
8. What Industrial occupations and trades are carried on—by males: and by females?—Males: basket, brush, mat and mattress making, weaving carpets. Females: brush making, chair caning, mattresses.
9. Are outdoor pupils received for instruction in trades, and up to what age?—Yes. Up to 40, if intelligent.
10. How many Blind employed in the workshops?—43.
11. Blind or sighted teachers? Are sighted workmen employed to assist in finishing blind work, or as journeymen?— Sighted. Deaf and Dumb where sight is required.
12. Is there a retail shop?—Yes.
13. If so, are goods not made by the Blind sold in it?—Yes.
14. What amount of goods were sold from the warehouse and retail shop last year, 1883?—4,400*l*.
15. When do the Managing Committee meet?—First Thursday in each month.
16. What were the subscriptions last year, 1883?—273*l*.
17. What were donations and legacies last year, 1883?—141*l*.
18. What income from endowments or trust funds?—None.
19. General remarks,-

BIRMINGHAM.

GENERAL INSTITUTION FOR THE BLIND,
EDGBASTON, BIRMINGHAM.

Honorary Secretaries . . { CHAS. RATCLIFF, Esq.
{ Mr. ALFRED KEEP.

1. Number of Blind in the Town?—About 400.
2. Objects of the Institution; if school, nature of Education?—To provide a resident school for the instruction of Blind children in the ordinary branches of education, with music, pianoforte tuning, and in trades; also workshops for adult non-resident Blind.
3. When founded?—1845.
4. What system of Reading in use?—Braille.
5. What number of male and female inmates, and amount charged (if any) for each?—Males, 42; females, 32. 10*l*. 10*s*. per year.
6. Age of admission, and how long they may remain?—10 to 21. Remain till they are proficient in their profession or trade if they behave well.
7. Qualification of Candidates for Admission?—Recommendation of a Governor, and engagement to pay the annual charge.
8. What Industrial occupations and trades are carried on—by males: and by females?—Basket work, chair cane seating, brush and mat making, knitting, crochet, &c.
9. Are outdoor pupils received for instruction in trades, and up to what age?
10. How many Blind employed in the workshops?—11.
11. Blind or sighted teachers? Are sighted workmen employed to assist in finishing blind work, or as journeymen?—Sighted head teachers, Blind assistants. No.
12. Is there a retail shop?—Yes: at the Institution.
13. If so, are goods not made by the Blind sold in it?—Yes.
14. What amount of goods were sold from the warehouse and retail shop last year, 1883?—1,890*l*.
15. When do the Managing Committee meet?—Second Thursday in the month.
16. What were the subscriptions last year, 1883?—660*l*.
17. What were donations and legacies last year, 1883?—1,515*l*.
18. What income from endowments or trust funds?—641*l*.
19. General remarks?

BRADFORD.

BRADFORD ASSOCIATION FOR IMPROVING THE SOCIAL CONDITION OF THE BLIND,

NORTH PARADE, BRADFORD.

Honorary Secretary . . Miss HOLLOWAY.

1. The number of Blind in the Town?—About 250.
2. Objects of the Institution; if school, nature of Education?—To provide workrooms for the Blind and instruction in trades; also a shop for the sale of goods, and a mission woman to visit the Blind at their homes, to teach reading, and to provide a lending library.
3. When founded?—1861.
4. What system of Reading in use?—Moon.
5. What number of male and female inmates, and amount charged (if any) for each?—Eight young women, for whom an exception has been made.
6. Age of admission, and how long they may remain?—Various ages; during good behaviour, and at the discretion of the Committee.
7. Qualification of Candidates for admission?—Loss of sight, and good character and needy circumstances.
8. What Industrial occupations and trades are carried on—by males: and by females?—Basket and brush making, chair caning, fancy matting.
9. Are outdoor pupils received for instruction in trades, and up to what age?—Yes.
10. How many Blind employed in the workshops?—65.
11. Blind or sighted teachers? Are sighted workmen employed to assist in finishing blind work, or as journeymen?—Sighted. Yes, both.
12. Is there a retail shop?—Yes.
13. If so, are goods not made by the Blind sold in it?—Yes.
14. What amount of goods were sold from the warehouse and retail shop last year, 1883?— 8,724*l*.
15. When do the Managing Committee meet?—First Wednesday in each month.
16. What were the subscriptions last year, 1883?— } 281*l*.
17. What were donations and legacies last year, 1883?—
18. What income from endowments or trust funds?—None.
19. General remarks.—

BRIGHTON.

BRIGHTON ASYLUM FOR THE INSTRUCTION OF THE BLIND,

EASTERN ROAD, BRIGHTON.

Honorary Secretary . . H. HEBBERT.

1. Number of Blind in the Town?
2. Objects of the Institution; if school, nature of Education?— To provide a resident school to give religious and general instruction to the Blind.
3. When founded?—1842.
4. What system of Reading in use?—Moon and Braille.
5. What number of male and female inmates, and amount charged (if any) for each?—18 boys and 16 girls, accommodation for 25 of each, average 12*l.* a year.
6. Age of admission, and how long they may remain?—Boys 8 to 18, girls 8 to 21; at the discretion of the Committee to keep them longer.
7. Qualification of Candidates for Admission?—Blindness.
8. What Industrial occupations and trades are carried on—by males: and by females?—Girls are taught worsted work and knitting, boys and girls basket work, vocal and instrumental music.
9. Are outdoor pupils received for instruction in trades, and up to what age?—Yes; of any age.
10. How many Blind employed in the workshops?—15 to 20.
11. Blind or sighted teachers? Are sighted workmen employed to assist in finishing blind work, or as journeymen?— Sighted teachers.
12. Is there a retail shop?—No, the goods made are sold in the town.
13. If so, are goods not made by the Blind sold in it?
14. What amount of goods were sold from the warehouse and retail shop last year, 1883?—31*l.*
15. When do the Managing Committee meet?—The second Tuesday in each month; except July and August.
16. What were the subscriptions last year, 1883?—286*l.*
17. What were donations and legacies last year, 1883?—223*l.*
18. What income from endowments or trust funds?—76*l.*
19. General remarks.—

BRISTOL.

BRISTOL ASYLUM OR SCHOOL OF INDUSTRY FOR THE BLIND,

QUEEN'S ROAD, PARK STREET, BRISTOL.

Secretary . . . Mr. GEORGE TAYLOR.

1. Number of Blind in the Town?
2. Objects of the Institution; if school, nature of Education?—To provide instruction in ordinary branches of education, with music, for the Blind, in a resident school, and also to teach the inmates trades, and to provide employment for non-resident Blind persons.
3. When founded?—1793.
4. What system of Reading in use?—Roman and Braille.
5. What number of male and female inmates, and amount charged (if any) for each?—32 males and 15 females. 5l. half-yearly in advance.
6. Age of admission, and how long they may remain?—9 to 21 for males, 2 to 25 for females. May remain seven years.
7. Qualification of Candidates for Admission?—Recommendation of a subscriber, and capacity to learn.
8. What Industrial occupations and trades are carried on—by males: and by females?—Basket work, mats, hearthrugs, wool work, chair seats.
9. Are outdoor pupils received for instruction in trades, and up to what age?—Yes.
10. How many Blind employed in the workshops?—11.
11. Blind or sighted teachers? Are sighted workmen employed to assist in finishing blind work, or as journeymen?—Blind teachers.
12. Is there a retail shop?—Yes: at the Institution.
13. If so, are goods not made by the Blind sold in it?
14. What amount of goods were sold from the warehouse and retail shop last year, 1883?—1,000l.
15. When do the Managing Committee meet?—Once a month.
16. What were the subscriptions last year, 1883?—212l.
17. What were donations and legacies last year, 1883?—675l.
18. What income from endowments or trust funds?—1,327l.
19. General remarks.—

BRISTOL.

BRISTOL AND CLIFTON ASSOCIATION FOR HOME TEACHING OF THE BLIND AND INDUSTRIAL EMPLOYMENT OF BLIND WOMEN AND GIRLS,

13 PARK ROW, BRISTOL.

Honorary Secretary . . Mrs. J. F. PERRY.

1. Number of Blind in the Town?—About 200 are known.
2. Objects of the Institution; if school, nature of Education?—To teach the Blind to read in their own homes, and women and girls to knit, and cane chairs at the Institution.
3. When founded?—1857.
4. What system of Reading in use?—Moon.
5. What number of male and female inmates, and amount charged (if any) for each?—None.
6. Age of admission, and how long they may remain?
7. Qualification of Candidates for Admission?—Blindness.
8. What Industrial occupations and trades are carried on—by males: and by females?—Knitting and chair caning.
9. Are outdoor pupils received for instruction in trades, and up to what age?—Yes, any age.
10. How many blind employed in the workshops?—16.
11. Blind or sighted teachers? Are sighted workmen employed to assist in finishing blind work, or as journeymen?—Blind teachers for home teaching; sighted for industrial work.
12. Is there a retail shop?—Yes.
13. If so, are goods not made by the Blind sold in it?—No.
14. What amount of goods were sold from the warehouse and retail shop last year?—220*l.* in 1882.
15. When do the Managing Committee meet?—The second Tuesday in each month.
16. What were the subscriptions last year?— } 217*l.* in 1882.
17. What were donations and legacies last year?— }
18. What income from endowments or trust funds?—24*l.*
19. General remarks.

BOLTON, LANCASHIRE.

BOLTON SCHOOLS AND WORKSHOPS FOR THE BLIND,
2 TIPPING STREET, BOLTON, LANCASHIRE.

Honorary Secretaries . . { A. GREG, Esq.
C. WOLFENDEN, Esq.

1. Number of Blind in the Town?
2. Objects of the Institution; if school, nature of Education?—To provide workshops for the Blind and instruction in trades, and to provide for the sale of the goods made by them; also to give instruction in reading.
3. When founded?—1867.
4. What system of Reading in use?—Moon.
5. What number of male and female inmates, and amount charged (if any) for each?—None.
6. Age of admission, and how long they may remain?
7. Qualification of Candidates for Admission?—Capacity for work, and good character.
8. What Industrial occupations and trades are carried on—by males: and by females?—Baskets, skips, mats, and brushes. The females make brushes and re-cane chairs.
9. Are outdoor pupils received for instruction in trades, and up to what age?—Yes; any age.
10. How many Blind employed in the workshops?—27 males and 4 females.
11. Blind or sighted teachers? Are sighted workmen employed to assist in finishing blind work, or as journeymen?—Blind teachers and sighted assistants.
12. Is there a retail shop?—No.
13. If so, are goods not made by the Blind sold in it?
14. What amount of goods were sold from the warehouse and retail shop last year, 1883?—2,301*l*.
15. When do the Managing Committee meet?—When required.
16. What were the subscriptions last year, 1883?—96*l*.
17. What were donations and legacies last year, 1883?—127*l*.
18. What income from endowments or trust funds?—58*l*.
19. General remarks.—

CARDIFF.

CARDIFF INSTITUTE FOR THE BLIND,
GLOSSOP ROAD, NEWPORT ROAD, CARDIFF.

Honorary Secretary . . Mr. G. F. WEBB.

1. Number of Blind in the Town?—About 70.
2. Objects of the Institution; if school, nature of Education?— To provide employment for the Blind and supply them with books, teach trades, &c.
3. When founded?—1865.
4. What system of Reading in use?—Moon.
5. What number of male and female inmates, and amount charged (if any) for each?
6. Age of admission, and how long they may remain?
7. Qualification of Candidates for Admission?—Ability to learn and work.
8. What Industrial occupations and trades are carried on—by males: and by females?—Basket making, mat making, and matting weaving; all by males.
9. Are outdoor pupils received for instruction in trades, and up to what age?— Yes; up to between 30 and 40 years.
10. How many Blind employed in the workshops?—24 men and lads.
11. Blind or sighted teachers? Are sighted workmen employed to assist in finishing blind work, or as journeymen?— Sighted. No.
12. Is there a retail shop?—Yes.
13. If so, are goods not made by the Blind sold in it?—Yes.
14. What amount of goods were sold from the warehouse and retail shop last year, 1883?—About 2,000*l.*
15. When do the Managing Committee meet?—About four times a year.
16. What were the subscriptions last year, 1883?
17. What were donations and legacies last year, 1883?
18. What income from endowments or trust funds?—None.
19. General remarks.—About 60*l.* a year is given for good conduct; also 3*s.* per week clear in addition to 50 per cent. towards a Sick Club in time of sickness, which Club is managed by the Blind themselves.

CARLISLE.

WORKSHOPS FOR THE BLIND OF CUMBERLAND AND WESTMORELAND,
LONSDALE STREET, CARLISLE.

Honorary Secretary . . Miss H. JOHNSON.

1. Number of Blind in the Town?—Town and district, 180.
2. Objects of the Institution; if school, nature of Education?—To teach the Blind trades, and to find them employment in workshops.
3. When founded?—1872.
4. What system of Reading in use?—Moon.
5. What number of male and female inmates, and amount charged (if any) for each?—6 workers are boarded in the Institution at a charge of 8s. per week.
6. Age of admission, and how long they may remain?—14. As long as Committee think well.
7. Qualification of Candidates for Admission?—Good character, and aptitude for work.
8. What Industrial occupations and trades are carried on—by males: and by females?—Men: basket making, matting, mats, and mattresses; women: chair seats and mattress cases.
9. Are outdoor pupils received for instruction in trades, and up to what age?—Yes. Any age from 14.
10. How many Blind employed in the workshops?—12 men and 2 women.
11. Blind or sighted teachers? Are sighted workmen employed to assist in finishing blind work, or as journeymen?—Sighted. Yes.
12. Is there a retail shop?—Yes.
13. If so, are goods not made by the Blind sold in it?—Yes.
14. What amount of goods were sold from the warehouse and retail shop last year, 1883?—1,625*l*.
15. When do the Managing Committee meet?—Monthly.
16. What were the subscriptions last year, 1883?—43*l*.
17. What were donations and legacies last year, 1883?—11*l*.
18. What income from endowments or trust funds?
19. General remarks.—The Home Teaching Society at Alston is now carried on by the Committee of this Institution.

CHELTENHAM.

CHELTENHAM AND GLOUCESTERSHIRE HOME TEACH-ING AND INDUSTRIAL SOCIETY FOR THE BLIND,
47 WINCHCOMB STREET, CHELTENHAM.

Honorary Secretary . . Rev. M. A. SMELT.

1. Number of Blind in the Town?—50.
2. Objects of the Institution; if school, nature of Education?—To provide workshops for the Blind, and to teach them trades, and to provide employment; also home teaching.
3. When founded?—1858.
4. What system of Reading in use?—Moon and Lucas.
5. What number of male and female inmates, and amount charged (if any) for each?—None.
6. Age of admission, and how long they may remain?
7. Qualification of Candidates for Admission?—Too blind for other employment.
8. What Industrial occupations and trades are carried on—by males: and by females?—Basket making, mat making, and knitting.
9. Are outdoor pupils received for instruction in trades, and up to what age?—Yes.
10. How many Blind employed in the workshops?—24 males, 12 females.
11. Blind or sighted teachers? Are sighted workmen employed to assist in finishing blind work, or as journeymen?—Blind teachers.
12. Is there a retail shop?—Yes.
13. If so, are goods not made by the Blind sold in it?—Yes, brushes.
14. What amount of goods were sold from the warehouse and retail shop last year, 1883?—465*l*.
15. When do the Managing Committee meet?—First Friday in the month.
16. What were the subscriptions last year, 1883?—130*l*.
17. What were donations and legacies last year, 1883?—25*l*.
18. What income from endowments or trust funds?
19. General remarks.—

CORK.

COUNTY AND CITY OF CORK ASYLUM FOR THE BLIND,

INFIRMARY ROAD, CORK, IRELAND.

Honorary Secretary . . F. W. ALLMAN.

1. Number of Blind in the Town?—About 100.
2. Objects of the Institution; if school, nature of Education?—To provide Homes for deserving Blind.
3. When founded?—1843.
4. What system of Reading in use?—Moon.
5. What number of male and female inmates, and amount charged (if any) for each?—49 females, 22 males; paid for by Aires Union in the County; 14*l.* per annum.
6. Age of admission, and how long they may remain?—Any age; no limit as to time.
7. Qualification of Candidates for Admission?—Good character, and freedom from chronic disorders.
8. What Industrial occupations and trades are carried on—by males: and by females?—Basket making, knitting, and household work by those with partial sight.
9. Are outdoor pupils received for instruction in trades, and up to what age?—No.
10. How many Blind employed in the workshops?—16 males, 30 females; the remainder are mostly invalids or employed in house work.
11. Blind or sighted teachers? Are sighted workmen employed to assist in finishing blind work, or as journeymen?—Sighted. No sighted workmen.
12. Is there a retail shop?—Yes.
13. If so, are goods not made by the Blind sold in it.—No.
14. What amount of goods were sold from the warehouse and retail shop last year, 1883?—226*l.*
15. When do the Managing Committee meet?—Each Wednesday.
16. What were the subscriptions last year, 1883?—233*l.*
17. What were donations and legacies last year, 1883?—325*l.*
18. What income from endowments or trust funds? 700*l.*
19. General remarks.—This is not a School, but simply a Home. Once admitted, the Blind seldom leave; some have been here more than thirty years.

DEVONPORT.

DEVONPORT AND WESTERN COUNTIES ASSOCIATION FOR THE BLIND,

ST. AUBYN STREET, DEVONPORT.

Honorary Secretary . . Rev. R. MILDREN, M.A.

1. Number of Blind in the Town?—About 50.
2. Objects of the Institution; if school, nature of Education?— To teach trades to the Blind; also reading and music; in a resident school.
3. When founded?—1860.
4. What system of Reading in use?—Moon.
5. What number of male and female inmates, and amount charged (if any) for each?—12 females and 10 males; from 3s. 6d. to 5s. per week.
6. Age of admission, and how long they may remain?—From 10 to 35; until able to maintain themselves.
7. Qualification of Candidates for Admission?—Guarantee of payment, good health, and capacity to learn.
8. What Industrial occupations and trades are carried on—by males; and by females?—Basket making, chair caning, knitting, sewing, and household duties.
9. Are outdoor pupils received for instruction in trades, and up to what age?
10. How many Blind employed in the workshops?—All.
11. Blind or sighted teachers? Are sighted workmen employed to assist in finishing blind work, or as journeymen?— Blind teachers.
12. Is there a retail shop?—Yes.
13. If so, are goods not made by the Blind sold in it?—Yes.
14. What amount of goods were sold from the warehouse and retail shop last year, 1883?—244*l*.
15. When do the Managing Committee meet?—First Monday in every month.
16. What were the subscriptions last year, 1883?—191*l*.
17. What were donations and legacies last year, 1883?—About 300*l*.
18. What income from endowments or trust funds?—About 100*l*.
19. General remarks.—

DUBLIN.

*THE RICHMOND NATIONAL INSTITUTION FOR THE BLIND,

41 UPPER SACKVILLE STREET, DUBLIN.

Secretary . .

1. Number of Blind in the Town?
2. Objects of the Institution; if school, nature of Education?—To provide a Protestant home for blind male children and adults, and instruction in trades.
3. When founded?—1810.
4. What system of Reading in use?
5. What number of male and female inmates, and amount charged (if any) for each?—A payment on entrance of £5.
6. Age of admission, and how long they may remain?—From 14 to 30; remain three years.
7. Qualification of Candidates for Admission?—Recommendation of subscriber.
8. What Industrial occupations and trades are carried on—by males: and by females?—Basket making, sack making, mat making, and net making.
9. Are outdoor pupils received for instruction in trades, and up to what age?
10. How many Blind employed in the workshops?
11. Blind or sighted teachers? Are sighted workmen employed to assist in finishing blind work, or as journeymen?
12. Is there a retail shop?
13. If so, are goods not made by the Blind sold in it?
14. What amount of goods were sold from the warehouse and retail shop last year, 1883?
15. When do the Managing Committee meet?
16. What were the subscriptions last year, 1883?
17. What were the donations and legacies last year, 1883?
18. What income from endowments or trust funds?
19. General remarks.—This institution is managed by Protestants, but Roman Catholics are received into it.

DUBLIN.

NATIONAL INSTITUTION AND MOLYNEUX ASYLUM FOR THE BLIND OF IRELAND,
LEESON PARK, DUBLIN.

Secretary . . EDWARD SMITH, Esq.

1. Number of Blind in the Town?
2. Objects of the Institution; if school, nature of Education?—To provide a Protestant school in which instruction shall be given in ordinary education and music; to teach blind female children; and provide a home for aged blind females. Printing and embossing are taught.
3. When founded?—1815.
4. What system of Reading in use?—Moon.
5. What number of male and female inmates, and amount charged (if any) for each?—55 females; in some cases £20 per annum.
6. Age of admission, and how long they may remain?—Five years and upwards. During good behaviour.
7. Qualification of Candidates for Admission?—Election by seat-holders of chapel; nomination of donor of £200; nomination of any person who guarantees £20 per annum; nomination of Poor Law Guardians under 6 and 7 Vict. cap. 92. sec. 14.
8. What Industrial occupations and trades are carried on—by males: and by females?—Printing and embossing, music, basket work, straw plaiting, chair caning, knitting, and netting.
9. Are outdoor pupils received for instruction in trades, and up to what age?—No.
10. How many Blind employed in the workshops?
11. Blind or sighted teachers? Are sighted workmen employed to assist in finishing blind work, or as journeymen?—Both.
12. Is there a retail shop?—Yes.
13. If so, are goods not made by the Blind sold in it?—Yes.
14. What amount of goods were sold from the warehouse and retail shop last year, 1883?—There is an annual sale of work at which work made by the inmates is sold. £56 received from the retail shop.
15. When do the Managing Committee meet?—Monthly.
16. What were the subscriptions last year, 1883?—£333.
17. What were the donations and legacies last year, 1883?—£727.
18. What income from endowments or trust funds?—£336.
19. General remarks.—

DUNDEE.

INSTITUTION FOR THE BLIND,
MAGDALEN GREEN, DUNDEE.

Honorary Secretary . . JAMES HUNTER, jun. Esq.

1. Number of Blind in the Town?—About 150.
2. Objects of the Institution; if school, nature of Education?—To provide workshops and give industrial employment, education, and teach music.
3. When founded?—1869.
4. What system of Reading in use?—Moon and Braille.
5. What number of male and female inmates, and amount charged (if any) for each?
6. Age of admission, and how long they may remain?—Admitted to workshops at 16.
7. Qualification of Candidates for Admission?—Blindness.
8. What Industrial occupations and trades are carried on—by males: and by females?—Basket making, brush making, mattress making, feather cleaning, weaving, firewood splitting by males. Mattress cover sewing, chair caning, and firewood bundling by females.
9. Are outdoor pupils received for instruction in trades, and up to what age?—Yes.
10. How many blind employed in the workshops?—54.
11. Blind or sighted teachers? Are sighted workmen employed to assist in finishing blind work, or as journeymen?—Sighted. Yes, as journeymen.
12. Is there a retail shop?—Yes.
13. If so, are goods not made by the Blind sold in it?—Yes.
14. What amount of goods were sold from the warehouse and retail shop last year, 1883?—At Institution, 3,178*l.* 11*s.* 1*d.* At shop, 1,240*l.* 11*s.* 2*d.*
15. When do the Managing Committee meet?—Monthly, on first Monday.
16. What were the subscriptions last year, 1883?—238*l.*
17. What were donations and legacies last year, 1883?—567*l.*
18. What income from endowments or trust funds?—147*l.*
19. General remarks.—In a few months the Institution is to be removed to new premises at Magdalen Green, the gift of the late Mrs. F. Malison, after which accommodation will be provided for residence.

EDINBURGH.

ROYAL BLIND ASYLUM AND SCHOOL,
NICOLSON STREET, EDINBURGH, AND WEST CRAIG MILLAR.

Secretary . . . . . W. F. CARTER.

1. Number of Blind in the Town?—500.
2. Objects of the Institution; if school, nature of Education?—To provide in a resident school instruction for blind children in ordinary branches of education and music, and an asylum for blind women. Also to teach trades and provide employment in workshops.
3. When founded?—1793.
4. What system of Reading in use?—Moon and Braille.
5. What number of male and female inmates, and amount charged (if any) for each?—30 females; 35 males. 10*l.* to 20*l.* per annum.
6. Age of admission, and how long they may remain?—5 years and upwards—remain for life.
7. Qualification of Candidates for Admission?—Health and capacity to work.
8. What Industrial occupations and trades are carried on—by males: and by females?
9. Are outdoor pupils received for instruction in trades, and up to what age?—Yes.
10. How many Blind employed in the workshops?—22 females, 114 males.
11. Blind or sighted teachers? Are sighted workmen employed to assist in finishing blind work, or as journeymen?—Sighted teachers.
12. Is there a retail shop?—Yes, two.
13. If so, are goods not made by the Blind sold in it?—Yes.
14. What amount of goods were sold from the warehouse and retail shop last year, 1883?—26,308*l.*
15. When do the Managing Committee meet?—Second Tuesday in the month.
16. What were the subscriptions last year, 1883?—1,533*l.*
17. What were donations and legacies last year, 1883?—5,727*l.*
18. What income from endowments or trust funds?—551*l.*
19. General remarks.—Some scholars are admitted free, and 16 scholarships have been recently founded, one by Her Gracious Majesty the Queen.

EXETER.

WEST OF ENGLAND INSTITUTION FOR THE BLIND,
ST. DAVID'S HILL, EXETER.

Honorary Secretary . . Rev. F. A. STEWART SAVILE.
Secretary . . . . WILLIAM TOWNSEND.

1. Number of Blind in the Town?—About 20.
2. Objects of the Institution; if school, nature of Education?—To provide instruction in ordinary branches of education and music for blind children and adults, in a resident school, and to provide instruction in trades and workshops for resident and non-resident Blind.
3. When founded?—1838.
4. What system of Reading in use?—Lucas, chiefly.
5. What number of male and female inmates, and amount charged (if any) for each?—21 males, 15 females. 4s. per week.
6. Age of admission, and how long they may remain?—8 to 18 years of age.
7. Qualification of Candidates for Admission?—Loss of useful sight.
8. What Industrial occupations and trades are carried on—by males: and by females?—Mat making, baskets, and sash-line by males. Basket making and knitting by females.
9. Are outdoor pupils received for instruction in trades, and up to what age?—Yes.
10. How many Blind employed in the workshops?—12.
11. Blind or sighted teachers? Are sighted workmen employed to assist in finishing blind work, or as journeymen?—Blind. 1 male sighted overseer. 1 female sighted overseer.
12. Is there a retail shop?—Yes.
13. If so, are goods not made by the Blind sold in it?—Brushes only.
14. What amount of goods were sold from the warehouse and retail shop last year, 1883?—804*l*.
15. When do the Managing Committee meet?—Monthly.
16. What were the subscriptions last year, 1883?—347*l*.
17. What were donations and legacies last year, 1883?—201*l*.
18. What income from endowments or trust funds?—169*l*.
19. General remarks.—

GLASGOW.

GLASGOW ASYLUM FOR THE BLIND,
102 CASTLE STREET, GLASGOW.

Honorary Secretary . . ROBERT JAMESON, Esq.

1. Number of Blind in the Town?—About 500.
2. Objects of the Institution; if school, nature of Education?— To provide instruction in ordinary branches of education, with music for blind women and boys in a resident school; also to provide instruction in trades for resident and non-resident pupils.
3. When founded?—1827.
4. What system of Reading in use?—Alston and Braille.
5. What number of male and female inmates, and amount charged (if any) for each?—34 males, 38 females. 12*l*. 12s. per annum.
6. Age of admission, and how long they may remain?—8 to 14 years, until education and apprenticeship are completed—say, average 7 years.
7. Qualification of Candidates for Admission?—Good character and sound constitution.
8. What Industrial occupations and trades are carried on—by males: and by females?—By males: sack weaving, twine spinning, basket making, mat making, mattress and bedding, brush making, and riddle making. Females: knitting, crochet, and mattress sewing.
9. Are outdoor pupils received for instruction in trades, and up to what age?—Yes; no fixed age, but as a rule not above 25.
10. How many Blind employed in the workshops?—76.
11. Blind or sighted teachers? Are sighted workmen employed to assist in finishing blind work, or as journeymen?—Both. Yes.
12. Is there a retail shop?—Yes, 2 shops.
13. If so, are goods not made by the Blind sold in it?—Yes.
14. What amount of goods were sold from the warehouse and retail shop last year, 1883?—3,114*l*.
15. When do the Managing Committee meet?—Second Tuesday of each month.
16. What were the subscriptions last year, 1883?—1,368*l*.
17. What were donations and legacies last year, 1883?—2,337*l*.
18. What income from endowments or trust funds?—539*l*.
19. General remarks.—

GREENWICH.

WORKSHOP FOR THE BLIND OF KENT,
1 SOUTH STREET, GREENWICH, S.E.

Honorary Secretary . . Major-General A. S. MOBERLY, R.E.

1. Number of Blind in the Town?
2. Objects of the Institution; if school, nature of Education?— To provide the Blind with instruction in trades, and to provide employment for the taught, in workshops, or in their own homes, without any machinery being required.
3. When founded?—1877.
4. What system of Reading in use?
5. What number of male and female inmates, and amount charged (if any) for each?
6. Age of admission, and how long they may remain?—Between the age of 15 and 40; at the discretion of the Committee.
7. Qualification of Candidates for Admission?—Some connection with the County of Kent, and being hopelessly blind.
8. What Industrial occupations and trades are carried on—by males: and by females?—Making of ship fendoffs, stuffing of life-buoy cushions with cork, basket making in all its branches, chair caning, and seating of ship-berths.
9. Are outdoor pupils received for instruction in trades, and up to what age?—Yes; up to 40.
10. How many Blind employed in the workshops?—12 to 14.
11. Blind or sighted teachers? Are sighted workmen employed to assist in finishing blind work, or as journeymen?— Both. The sighted teacher assists in finishing.
12. Is there a retail shop?—Yes.
13. If so, are goods not made by the Blind sold in it?—No.
14. What amount of goods were sold from the warehouse and retail shop last year, 1883?—790*l*.
15. When do the Managing Committee meet?—On Tuesdays, Thursdays, and Saturdays throughout the year.
16. What were the subscriptions last year, 1883?—
17. What were donations and legacies last year, 1883?— } 364*l*.
18. What income from endowments or trust funds?—None.
19. General remarks.—The teaching has to be paid for either by the guardians of the poor, or by friends of the blind man.

HULL.

HULL BLIND INSTITUTION,

KINGSTON SQUARE, HULL.

Honorary Secretary . . T. PRIESTMAN, Esq.

1. Number of Blind in the Town?—About 200.
2. Objects of the Institution; if school, nature of Education?— To provide workshops for the Blind, and instruction in trades and employment, to instruct the Blind at their own homes to read, and to supply them with books.
3. When founded?—1868.
4. What system of Reading in use?—Moon.
5. What number of male and female inmates, and amount charged (if any) for each?—None.
6. Age of admission, and how long they may remain?—Any age, any time.
7. Qualification of Candidates for Admission?—Good character, health, and capacity to learn.
8. What Industrial occupations and trades are carried on—by males: and by females?—Basket making.
9. Are outdoor pupils received for instruction in trades, and up to what age?—Yes; any age.
10. How many Blind employed in the workshops?—14.
11. Blind or sighted teachers? Are sighted workmen employed to assist in finishing blind work, or as journeymen?— Sighted teachers for trade; 2 sighted journeymen.
12. Is there a retail shop?—No.
13. If so, are goods not made by the Blind sold in it?
14. What amount of goods were sold from the warehouse last year?—459*l*. in 1882.
15. When do the Managing Committee meet?—Not fixed.
16. What were the subscriptions last year?— } 115*l*. in 1882.
17. What were donations and legacies last year?—
18. What income from endowments or trust funds?—14*l*.
19. General remarks.—The Institution is about to be enlarged and reorganised, and a retail shop added.

INVERNESS.

NORTHERN COUNTIES INSTITUTE FOR THE BLIND,
81 CASTLE STREET, INVERNESS.

Honorary Secretary . . Hugh Rose, Esq.

1. Number of Blind in the Town?—423 in the counties embraced by the Institution, viz. Inverness, Nairn, Elgin, Ross, Sutherland, Caithness, and Orkney.
2. Objects of the Institution; if school, nature of Education?—To educate blind children (in ordinary branches of education), to provide Industrial employment for the Blind, and to visit and teach the Blind in their own home.
3. When founded?—1866.
4. What system of Reading in use?—Moon and Braille.
5. What number of male and female inmates, and amount charged (if any) for each?—Male inmates in Educational home 5; Female do. 7; 10*l.* per annum.
6. Age of admission, and how long they may remain?—8 to 16, female pupils.
7. Qualification of Candidates for Admission?
8. What Industrial occupations and trades are carried on—by males: and by females?—Males: bedding, basket making, and making of sheep mats. Females: sewing and knitting.
9. Are outdoor pupils received for instruction in trades, and up to what age?—Yes; no fixed age.
10. How many Blind employed in the workshops?—6 males.
11. Blind or sighted teachers? Are sighted workmen employed to assist in finishing blind work, or as journeymen?—Blind teachers (female) in school, sighted in workshop.
12. Is there a retail shop?—Yes.
13. If so, are goods not made by the Blind sold in it?—Yes, but baskets only.
14. What amount of goods were sold from the warehouse and retail shop last year, 1883?—592*l.*
15. When do the Managing Committee meet?—Every week.
16. What were the subscriptions last year, 1883?—347*l.*
17. What were donations and legacies last year, 1883?—99*l.*
18. What income from endowments or trust funds?—None.
19. General remarks.—

LEEDS.

UNITED INSTITUTION FOR THE BLIND AND DEAF AND DUMB,

ALBION STREET, LEEDS.

Honorary Secretary . . THOMAS HARVEY, Esq.

1. Number of Blind in the Town?
2. Objects of the Institution; if school, nature of Education?— To provide workshops for the Blind: to maintain a school for children (Blind): to provide rooms for the Deaf and Dumb, and to encourage their secular and religious education: to visit the sick and infirm Blind and Mutes, and to assist them in finding employment, &c.
3. When founded?—1866.
4. What system of reading in use?—Moon and Braille.
5. What number of male and female inmates, and amount charged (if any) for each?—16 children, male and female (3s. 6d. per week). Day scholars, male and female, 16. Education and dinner, 4d. per week. The children are taught singing, and some instrumental music.
6. Age of admission, and how long they may remain?—Children between 5 and 15 to school.
7. Qualification of Candidates for Admission?—Health and capacity to learn, 6 months' residence in the Borough, and good character.
8. What Industrial occupations and trades are carried on—by males: and by females?—Brush making, basket making, chair caning, and knitting.
9. Are outdoor pupils received for instruction in trades, and up to what age?—Yes; discretion of Committee.
10. How many Blind employed in the workshops?—34.
11. Blind or sighted teachers? Are sighted workmen employed to assist in finishing blind work, or as journeymen?— Sighted workmen are employed as journeymen.
12. Is there a retail shop?—Yes.
13. If so, are goods not made by the Blind sold in it?—Yes.
14. What amount of goods were sold from the warehouse and retail shop last year, 1883?—3,248l.
15. When do the Managing Committe meet?—Once a month.
16. What were the subscriptions last year, 1883?—503l.
17. What were donations and legacies last year, 1883? 55l.
18. What income from endowments or trust funds?—None.
19. General remarks.

LEICESTER.

LEICESTER ASSOCIATION FOR PROMOTING THE GENERAL WELFARE OF THE BLIND,

42 GRANBY STREET, LEICESTER.

Honorary Secretary . . S. HARRIS, Esq.

1. Number of Blind in the Town?—About 125.
2. Objects of the Institution; if school, nature of Education?—To provide workshops for the Blind, and to instruct them in trades, and provide them with constant employment. To provide a teacher to visit the Blind at their homes, and teach them to read, and to supply them with books.
3. When founded?—1858.
4. What system of Reading in use?—Moon, Braille.
5. What number of male and female inmates, and amount charged (if any) for each?—None.
6. Age of admission, and how long they may remain?
7. Qualification of Candidates for Admission?—Health and capacity to learn.
8. What Industrial occupations and trades are carried on—by males: and by females?—By the men: the manufacture of basket work, and re-seating chairs with rushes and willow. By the women: brush drawing, and cane-chair re-seating.
9. Are outdoor pupils received for instruction in trades, and up to what age?—Yes.
10. How many Blind employed in the workshops?—25.
11. Blind or sighted teachers? Are sighted workmen employed to assist in finishing blind work, or as journeymen?—Sighted, employed in both capacities.
12. Is there a retail shop?—Yes.
13. If so, are goods not made by the Blind sold in it?—Yes.
14. What amount of goods were sold from the warehouse and retail shop last year, 1883?—From warehouse, 789*l.* 2*s.*; from shop, 1,878*l.* 6*s.* 11*d.*
15. When do the Managing Committee meet?—Every Wednesday.
16. What were the subscriptions last year, 1883?—136*l.*
17. What were donations and legacies last year, 1883?—211*l.*
18. What income from endowments or trust funds?—None.
19. General remarks.—New premises were opened in 1882, and business considerably increased. There is a cottage home provided for aged and infirm Blind.

LIVERPOOL.

SCHOOL FOR THE BLIND,
HARDMAN STREET, LIVERPOOL.

Honorary Secretary . .

1. Number of Blind in the Town?—About 650.
2. Objects of the Institution; if school, nature of Education?—To provide instruction for the Blind in the ordinary branches of education; to teach trade work, and where aptitude is discerned, both vocal and instrumental music.
3. When founded?—1791.
4. What system of Reading in use?—Moon, Roman, and Braille.
5. What number of male and female inmates, and amount charged (if any) for each?—50 males, 36 females; 4s. 6d. per week.
6. Age of admission, and how long they may remain?—Females 12, males 14; remain 6 years.
7. Qualification of Candidates for Admission?—Health, capacity, and payment.
8. What Industrial occupations are carried on—by males: and by females?—Basket and mat making, and chair caning.
9. Are outdoor pupils received for instruction in trades, and up to what age?—Yes, up to 45 years of age.
10. How many Blind employed in the workshops?—53.
11. Blind or sighted teachers? Are sighted workmen employed to assist in finishing blind work, or as journeymen?—Sighted teachers, who assist in finishing.
12. Is there a retail shop?—Yes.
13. If so, are goods not made by the Blind sold in it?—Yes.
14. What amount of goods were sold from the warehouse and retail shop last year, 1883?—900*l*.
15. When do the Managing Committee meet?—The first Tuesday in every month.
16. What were the subscriptions last year, 1883?—535*l*.
17. What were donations and legacies last year, 1883?—Not given.
18. What income from endowments or trust funds?—552*l*.
19. General remarks.—This is the oldest school for the Blind in the Kingdom. It has (like most of the old schools) a chapel attached to it, the pew-rents of which form part of its permanent income. At this Institution the inmates wear a distinctive dress.

LIVERPOOL.

LIVERPOOL WORKSHOPS AND HOME TEACHING SOCIETY FOR THE OUTDOOR BLIND,
CORNWALLIS STREET, LIVERPOOL.

Honorary Secretary . WALTER J. CHAMBERS, Esq.

1. Number of Blind in the Town?—600 to 700.
2. Objects of the Institution; if school, nature of Education?— To provide workshops for the Blind, and to instruct them in trades, and give them employment; also to provide for the visitation of the Blind at their homes, and give instruction in reading.
3. When founded?—1860.
4. What system of Reading in use?—Moon.
5. What number of male and female inmates, and amount charged (if any) for each?
6. Age of admission, and how long may they remain?—May enter as soon as old enough to learn a trade, and remain as long as able to work at it.
7. Qualification of Candidates for Admission?—Blindness; 12 months' residence in Liverpool prior to application; good character.
8. What Industrial occupations and trades are carried on—by males: and by females?—By men: mat making in all branches, basket making, brush making, mattress making, &c. By women: knitting, sewing, mattress making, brush making.
9. Are outdoor pupils received for instruction in trades, and up to what age?—As apprentices preferably while young, but sometimes up to 30 or 40 years of age.
10. How many Blind employed in the workshops?—126.
11. Blind or sighted teachers? Are sighted workmen employed to assist in finishing blind work, or as journeymen?— Sighted teachers and foremen. Sighted workmen employed for such portions of the work as cannot be done to advantage by the Blind.
12. Is there a retail shop?—Yes.
13. If so, are goods not made by the Blind sold in it?—Yes.
14. What amount of goods were sold from the warehouse and retail shop last year, 1883?—13,138*l.*
15. When do the Managing Committee meet?—The second Wednesday or Friday in each month.
16. What were the subscriptions last year, 1883?—354*l.* to workshops (about 200*l.* in all for Home Teaching Branch).

17. What were donations and legacies last year, 1883?—674*l*.
18. What income from endowments or trust funds?—64*l*.
19. General remarks.—

LIVERPOOL.

CATHOLIC BLIND ASYLUM,
59 BRUNSWICK ROAD, LIVERPOOL.

Honorary Secretary . . PAUL CULLEN.

1. Number of Blind in the Town?
2. Objects of the Institution; if school, nature of Education?—To provide instruction for blind Catholics in the ordinary branches of education, with music, in a resident school.
3. When founded?—1841.
4. What system of Reading in use?—Braille.
5. What number of male and female inmates, and amount charged (if any) for each?—68; 3*s*. 6*d*. per week for some pupils.
6. Age of admission, and how long they may remain?—10 years, occasionally younger.
7. Qualifications of Candidates for Admission?—Health, capacity to learn, and register of Baptism.
8. What Industrial occupations and trades are carried on—by males; and by females?—Manufacture of basket work, mats, matting, hearthrugs, brushes, sash cords, knitting, caning chairs, &c.
9. Are outdoor pupils received for instruction in trades, and up to what age?
10. How many Blind employed in the workshops?—68.
11. Blind or sighted teachers? Are sighted workmen employed to assist in finishing blind work, or as journeymen?—Sighted teachers.
12. Is there a retail shop?—Yes.
13. If so, are goods not made by the Blind sold in it?—Yes.
14. What amount of goods were sold from the warehouse and retail shop last year, 1883?—307*l*.
15. When do the Managing Committee meet?—Monthly.
16. What were the subscriptions last year, 1883?—173*l*.
17. What were donations and legacies last year, 1883?
18. What income from endowments or trust funds?—50*l*.
19. General remarks.—New building just finished.

LONDON.

SCHOOL FOR THE INDIGENT BLIND,
ST. GEORGE'S FIELDS, SOUTHWARK, LONDON, S.E.

Secretary . . . . Rev. B. G. Johns, M.A.

1. Number of Blind in the Town?—About 300.
2. Objects of the Institution; if school, nature of Education?—To provide instruction for blind children in ordinary branches of education, with music, in a resident school, and to teach them trades; also to employ non-resident blind adults.
3. When founded?—1799.
4. What system of Reading in use?—Roman chiefly. Other systems are used if found advisable.
5. What number of male and female inmates, and amount charged (if any) for each?—180. No charge.
6. Age of admission, and how long they may remain?—7 to 20. Remain 6 years.
7. Qualification of Candidates for Admission?—Good character, health, and capacity to learn.
8. What Industrial occupations and trades are carried on—by males: and by females?—Basket work, mats, matting, hearthrugs, brushes, sash-line, netting, and knitting.
9. Are outdoor pupils received for instruction in trades, and up to what age?—Yes.
10. How many Blind employed in the workshops?—28.
11. Blind or sighted teachers? Are sighted workmen employed to assist in finishing blind work, or as journeymen?—Sighted teachers.
12. Is there a retail shop?—Goods are sold at the Institution.
13. If so, are goods not made by the Blind sold in it?—No.
14. What amount of goods were sold from the warehouse and retail shop last year, 1883?—3,272*l*.
15. When do the Managing Committee meet?
16. What were the subscriptions last year, 1883?—835*l*.
17. What were donations and legacies last year, 1883?—2,986*l*.
18. What income from endowments or trust funds?—4,685*l*.
19. General remarks.—There is a Junior Branch School, London Lodge, Wandsworth Common, S.W.

LONDON.

LONDON SOCIETY FOR TEACHING THE BLIND TO READ, ETC.,

UPPER AVENUE ROAD, REGENT'S PARK, LONDON, N.W.

Honorary Treasurer . . J. HORNSBY WRIGHT, ESQ.

---

1. Number of Blind in the Town?
2. Objects of the Institution; if school, nature of Education?—To provide instruction for the Blind in ordinary branches of education, with music, in a resident school; also to teach the Blind trades.
3. When founded?—1838.
4. What system of Reading in use?—Lucas and Braille.
5. What number of male and female inmates, and amount charged (if any) for each?—Male, 29; female, 25. 15*l.* to 35*l.* for boarders per annum. 30*s.* for day pupils per annum.
6. Age of admission, and how long they may remain?—Males, 8 to 17; females, 8 to 20.
7. Qualification of Candidates for Admission?—Health, and capacity to learn.
8. What Industrial occupations and trades are carried on—by males: and by females?—By males: printing Lucas books, basket making, chair caning. Females: knitting.
9. Are outdoor pupils received for instruction in trades, and up to what age?—No.
10. How many Blind employed in the workshops?
11. Blind or sighted teachers? Are sighted workmen employed to assist in finishing blind work, or as journeymen?—Both.
12. Is there a retail shop?—Yes, at the Institution.
13. If so, are goods not made by the Blind sold in it?
14. What amount of goods were sold from the warehouse and retail shop last year, 1883?—52*l.*
15. When do the Managing Committee meet?—Second Monday in each month.
16. What were the subscriptions last year, 1883?—483*l.*
17. What were donations and legacies last year, 1883?—1,438*l.*
18. What income from endowments or trust funds?—44*l.*
19. General remarks.—

LONDON.

ASSOCIATION FOR PROMOTING THE GENERAL WELFARE OF THE BLIND,

28 BERNERS STREET, LONDON.

Honorary Secretary . . HUME NICHOLL, Esq.

1. Number of Blind in the Town?—About 3,000.
2. Objects of the Institution; if school, nature of Education?—To provide workshops for the Blind, and instruction in trades, and employment; and to promote the general welfare of the Blind.
3. When founded?—1856.
4. What system of Reading in use?—None.
5. What number of male and female inmates, and amount charged (if any) for each?—None.
6. Age of admission, and how long they may remain?
7. Qualification of Candidates for Admission?—Health, and capacity to learn.
8. What Industrial occupations and trades are carried on—by males: and by females?—Males: baskets, brushes, mats, sacks, firewood. Females: chair caning, brush making, sash-lines, wool work.
9. Are outdoor pupils received for instruction in trades, and up to what age?—Yes. All adults.
10. How many Blind employed in the workshops?—47.
11. Blind or sighted teachers? Are sighted workmen employed to assist in finishing blind work, or as journeymen?—Blind teachers. Sighted workmen are employed.
12. Is there a retail shop?—Yes.
13. If so, are goods not made by the Blind sold in it?—Yes.
14. What amount of goods were sold from the warehouse and retail shop last year, 1883?—8,461*l*.
15. When do the Managing Committee meet?
16. What were the subscriptions last year, 1883?—729*l*.
17. What were donations and legacies last year, 1883?—2,964*l*.
18. What income from endowments or trust funds?—646*l*.
19. General remarks.—In addition to wages earned, all the women employed receive 1*s*. per week as a gift.

LONDON.

ROYAL NORMAL COLLEGE AND ACADEMY OF MUSIC FOR THE BLIND,

WESTOW STREET, UPPER NORWOOD, S.E.

Honorary Secretary . Major CAVENDISH C. FITZROY.

1. Number of Blind in the Town?
2. Objects of the Institution; if school, nature of Education?—To provide a resident school for the instruction of the Blind in general education, in the training of the teachers (especially of the Blind) in the science and practice of music, and in pianoforte tuning.
3. When founded?—1872.
4. What system of Reading in use?—Braille.
5. What number of male and female inmates, and amount charged (if any) for each?—98 males; 65 females.
6. Age of admission, and how long they may remain?—Primary school from 7 to 12, to stay 1 to 3 years. College 9 to 21, to stay from 3 to 6 years. The technical school, under 25 years, to stay from 2 to 4 years.
7. Qualification of Candidates for Admission?—In the primary school, ability to learn. In the college, ability to read and write Braille type, with good fundamental knowledge of arithmetic and English grammar, and to be prepared for the work of the platform. (See Report.)
8. What Industrial occupations and trades are carried on—by males: and by females?—Males: pianoforte tuning and repairing, training for teaching literature and music, training for organists and choirmasters. Females: knitting, sewing, &c.
9. Are outdoor pupils received for instruction in trades, and up to what age?—No.
10. How many Blind employed in the workshops?
11. Blind or sighted teachers? Are sighted workmen employed to assist in finishing blind work, or as journeymen?
12. Is there a retail shop?
13. If so, are goods not made by the Blind sold in it?
14. What amount of goods were sold from the warehouse and retail shop last year, 1883?
15. When do the Managing Committee meet?—Second Tuesday in each month.
16. What were the subscriptions last year, 1883?—7,636*l.*

17. What were donations and legacies last year, 1883?—4,302*l*.
18. What income from endowments or trust funds?
19. General remarks.—Physical education and training receive great attention; gymnasiums for both sexes, with swimming baths, have been set up, and large playgrounds afford all possible means of enjoying games and exercises by the pupils.

LONDON.

KENSINGTON INSTITUTE FOR THE BLIND,
2 YOUNG STREET, KENSINGTON, W.

Honorary Secretary . . H. R. KNIPE, Esq.

1. Number of Blind in the Town?
2. Objects of the Institution; if school, nature of Education?—To provide work and workshops for the industrial blind poor, and to give instruction in trades to poor blind persons.
3. When founded?—1881.
4. What system of Reading in use?
5. What number of male and female inmates, and amount charged (if any) for each?
6. Age of admission, and how long they may remain?
7. Qualification of Candidates for Admission?—Total blindness.
8. What Industrial occupations and trades are carried on—by males; and by females?—Brush and basket making by males. Chair caning by females.
9. Are outdoor pupils received for instruction in trades, and up to what age?—Yes; no limit as to age.
10. How many Blind employed in the workshops?—10.
11. Blind or sighted teachers? Are sighted workmen employed to assist in finishing blind work, or as journeymen?—Both. Yes.
12. Is there a retail shop?—Yes.
13. If so, are goods not made by the Blind sold in it?—Yes.
14. What amount of goods were sold from the warehouse and retail shop last year, 1883?—761*l*.
15. When do the Managing Committee meet?—Every Saturday.
16. What were the subscriptions last year, 1883?—78*l*.
17. What were donations and legacies last year, 1883?—419*l*.
18. What income from endowments or trust funds?—Nil.
19. General remarks.—

LONDON.

HOME FOR BLIND CHILDREN,

GOLDSMITH'S PLACE, KILBURN PRIORY, LONDON, N.W.

Honorary Secretary . . Miss E. F. NEWBERY.

1. Number of Blind in the Town?
2. Objects of the Institution; if school, nature of Education?—To provide instruction in ordinary branches of education, with music, for blind children in a resident school.
3. When founded?—1869.
4. What system of Reading in use?—Moon and Braille.
5. What number of male and female inmates, and amount charged (if any) for each?—8 males, 18 females. 12*l*. 10*s*., and 2*l*. extra for music.
6. Age of admission, and how long they may remain?—Admission 3 to 8. Boys remain till 12. Girls any time.
7. Qualification of Candidates for Admission?—Health and capacity.
8. What Industrial occupations and trades are carried on—by males: and by females?—Chair caning for all. Knitting and sewing for girls, and making mats and balls for younger children.
9. Are outdoor pupils received for instruction in trades, and up to what age?—No.
10. How many Blind employed in the workshops?
11. Blind or sighted teachers? Are sighted workmen employed to assist in finishing blind work, or as journeymen?—One sighted teacher, one blind.
12. Is there a retail shop?—No.
13. If so, are goods not made by the Blind sold in it?
14. What amount of goods were sold from the warehouse and retail shop last year, 1883?
15. When do the Managing Committee meet?—There is no Committee.
16. What were the subscriptions last year, 1883?—108*l*.
17. What were donations and legacies last year, 1883?—239*l*.
18. What income from endowments or trust funds?
19. General remarks.

MANCHESTER.

HENSHAW'S BLIND ASYLUM, OUTDOOR WORKSHOPS,
BLOOM STREET, SALFORD.

Secretary . J. W. RATTRAY.

1. Number of Blind in the Town (Manchester and Salford)?—450.
2. Objects of the Institution?—To employ blind persons who have learnt a trade.
3. When founded?—1881. Taken over by Henshaw's Charity, January 1883.
4. What system of reading in use?
5. What number of males and females employed?—18 males; no females.
6. Age of admission, and how long they may remain?—Adults; during good behaviour.
7. Qualification of Candidates for Admission?—Having learned a trade.
8. What Industrial occupations and trades are carried on—by males?—Basket making, mats and matting weaving, chair seating, and upholstery.
9. Are outdoor pupils received for instruction in trades, and up to what age?—No.
10. How many Blind employed in the workshops?—18.
11. Blind or sighted teachers? Are sighted workmen employed to assist in finishing blind work, or as journeymen?—Sighted foreman, who finishes.
12. Is there a retail shop?—Yes.
13. If so, are goods not made by the Blind sold in it?—Yes.
14. What amount of goods were sold from the warehouse and retail shop last year, 1883?—1,509*l*.
15. When do the Managing Committee meet?—Fortnightly.
16. What were the subscriptions last year, 1883?—Included in accounts of Henshaw's Manchester Asylum.
17. What were donations and legacies last year, 1883?—Included in accounts of Henshaw's Manchester Asylum.
18. What income from endowments or trust funds?—Included in accounts of Henshaw's Manchester Asylum.
19. General remarks.—This Institution, now managed by Henshaw's Blind Asylum Board, is carried on where their predecessors established it, in Bloom Street, Salford.

MANCHESTER.

HENSHAW'S BLIND ASYLUM,
OLD TRAFFORD, MANCHESTER.

Secretary . . . . J. W. RATTRAY.

1. Number of Blind in the Town?
2. Objects of the Institution; if school, nature of Education?—
   To afford an Asylum for the impotent and aged Blind, and to maintain and afford such instruction to the indigent Blind of both sexes capable of employment as will enable them to provide either wholly or in part for their own subsistence, and to promote the employment of or to employ blind persons.
3. When founded?—1827.
4. What system of Reading in use?—Moon and Braille.
5. What number of male and female inmates, and amount charged (if any) for each?—77 males and 43 females; from 3s. to 6s. each per week.
6. Age of admission, and how long they may remain?—Females for life. Males 7 years.
7. Qualification of Candidates for Admission?—Blindness; good character.
8. What Industrial occupations and trades are carried on—by males: and by females?—Males: mats, matting, and baskets. Females: knitting, sewing, &c.
9. Are outdoor pupils received for instruction in trades, and up to what age?
10. How many Blind employed in the workshops?—All over 16 years of age, except music pupils.
11. Blind or sighted teachers? Are sighted workmen employed to assist in finishing blind work, or as journeymen?—Both.
12. Is there a retail shop?—Yes.
13. If so, are goods not made by the Blind sold in it?—Yes.
14. What amount of goods were sold from the warehouse and retail shop last year, 1883?—502*l*.
15. When do the Managing Committee meet?—Fortnightly.
16. What were the subscriptions last year, 1883?—107*l*.
17. What were donations and legacies last year, 1883?—9,035*l*.
18. What income from endowments or trust funds?—1,764*l*.
19. General remarks.—

NEWCASTLE-ON-TYNE.

ROYAL VICTORIA ASYLUM FOR THE BLIND,
79 NORTHUMBERLAND STREET, NEWCASTLE-ON-TYNE.

Honorary Secretaries . . { JOHN T. DOBSON.
{ THOMAS YOUNG.

1. Number of Blind in the Town?
2. Objects of the Institution; if school, nature of Education?—To provide instruction in ordinary branches of education, with music, for the Blind; also to teach them trades in a resident school.
3. When founded?—1838.
4. What system of Reading in use?—Moon and Braille.
5. What number of male and female inmates, and amount charged (if any) for each?—25 males; 18 females. 10*l*. 10*s*. yearly.
6. Age of admission, and how long they may remain?—7 years. From 2 to 7 years.
7. Qualification of Candidates?—Residence in one of the four Northern counties.
8. What Industrial occupations and trades are carried on—by males: and by females?—Males: basket making, mat making, mattress making. Females: knitting and sewing.
9. Are outdoor pupils received for instruction in trades, and up to what age?
10. How many Blind employed in the workshops?—The pupils and their teachers, 3 in number.
11. Blind or sighted teachers? Are sighted workmen employed to assist in finishing blind work, or as journeymen?—Both. No.
12. Is there a retail shop?—Yes, at the Institution.
13. If so, are goods not made by the Blind sold in it?—Yes.
14. What amount of goods were sold from the warehouse and retail shop last year, 1883?—190*l*.
15. When do the Managing Committee meet?—Monthly.
16. What were the subscriptions last year, 1883?—172*l*.
17. What were donations and legacies last year, 1883?—1,711*l*.
18. What income from endowments or trust funds? 254*l*.
19. General remarks.

NEWCASTLE-ON-TYNE.

WORKSHOPS FOR THE BLIND,

59 BLACKETT STREET, NEWCASTLE-ON-TYNE.

Honorary Secretaries . . { W. GOODE DAVIES, Esq.
{ Rev. W. B. EAST.

1. Number of Blind in the Town?—About 120.
2. Objects of the Institution; if school, nature of Education?—To provide workshops for the Blind, and to provide them with employment.
3. When founded?—1870.
4. What system of Reading in use?
5. What number of male and female inmates, and amount charged (if any) for each?
6. Age of admission, and how long they may remain?
7. Qualification of Candidates for Admission?—Health and capacity to work.
8. What Industrial occupations and trades are carried on—by males: and by females?—Mattress making.
9. Are outdoor pupils received for instruction in trades, and up to what age?
10. How many Blind employed in the workshops?
11. Blind or sighted teachers? Are sighted workmen employed to assist in finishing blind work, or as journeymen?—Sighted teachers.
12. Is there a retail shop?—Yes.
13. If so, are goods not made by the Blind sold in it?
14. What amount of goods were sold from the warehouse and retail shop last year, 1883?
15. When do the Managing Committee meet?
16. What were the subscriptions last year, 1883?
17. What were donations and legacies last year, 1883?
18. What income from endowments or trust funds?
19. General remarks.—

NORWICH.

ASYLUM AND SCHOOL FOR THE BLIND,
NORWICH.

Secretary . THOMAS G. BAYFIELD.

1. Number of Blind in the Town?
2. Objects of the Institution; if school, nature of Education?—To provide a home for the aged Blind, instruction in ordinary branches of education and music for children in a resident school, and to teach them trades.
3. When founded?—1805.
4. What system of Reading in use?—Moon and Roman capitals.
5. What number of male and female inmates, and amount charged (if any) for each?—4 aged men, 7 aged women; 19 male pupils, 16 female pupils. The rate of payment fixed by Committee.
6. Age of admission, and how long they may remain?—Aged Blind, 55 years and upwards. For children, as pupils, 10 years.
7. Qualification of Candidates for Admission?—For the aged Blind, good character. For Blind children, health and capacity to work.
8. What Industrial occupations and trades are carried on—by males: and by females?—Males: baskets, mats, matting, hearthrugs, sacks, bottle envelopes. Females: knitting.
9. Are outdoor pupils received for instruction in trades, and up to what age?
10. How many Blind employed in the workshops?—4 blind journeymen in mat shops and 2 in basket shop. 4 pupils in mat shops and 14 pupils in basket shop.
11. Blind or sighted teachers? Are sighted workmen employed to assist in finishing blind work, or as journeymen?—Sighted teachers.
12. Is there a retail shop?—Yes.
13. If so, are goods not made by the Blind sold in it?—No.
14. What amount of goods were sold from the warehouse and retail shop last year, 1883?—484*l*.
15. When do the Managing Committee meet?—Third Tuesday in the month.
16. What were the subscriptions last year, 1883?—251*l*.

17. What were donations and legacies last year, 1883?—218*l*.
18. What income from endowments or trust funds?—443*l*.
19. General remarks.—

NOTTINGHAM.

MIDLAND INSTITUTION FOR THE BLIND,
CLARENDON STREET, NOTTINGHAM.

Honorary Secretary . . Mr. H. L. SWIFT.

1. Number of Blind in the Town?
2. Objects of the Institution; if school, nature of Education?— To provide instruction in the ordinary branches of education, with music, for blind children in a resident school, and to teach them trades; also to provide non-resident blind adults with employment.
3. When founded?—1843.
4. What system of Reading in use?—Braille.
5. What number of male and female inmates, and amount charged (if any) for each?—27 males and 28 females. Indoor, 5*l*. 17*s*. per half-year.
6. Age of admission, and how long they may remain?—7 years old. No fixed time to remain.
7. Qualification of Candidates for Admission?—Recommendation of governor, health, and capacity.
8. What Industrial occupations and trades are carried on—by males: and by females?—The manufacture of basket work, mats, matting, brushes, mops, mattresses, hearthrugs, chair seats, crochet and knitted articles, with sewing.
9. Are outdoor pupils received for instruction in trades, and up to what age?—Yes. Any age.
10. How many Blind employed in the workshops?—21.
11. Blind or sighted teachers?—Are sighted workmen employed to assist in finishing blind work, or as journeymen?— Sighted teachers. No.
12. Is there a retail shop?—Yes.
13. If so, are goods not made by the Blind sold in it?—Yes.
14. What amount of goods were sold from the warehouse and retail shop last year, 1883?—1,700*l*.
15. When do the Managing Committee meet?—Last Tuesday in each month.
16. What were the subscriptions last year, 1883?—Collected, 539*l*.

17. What were donations and legacies last year, 1883?—1,285*l*.
18. What income from endowments or trust funds?—189*l*.
19. General remarks.—A gymnasium has lately been added.

PECKHAM.

SURREY ASSOCIATION FOR THE GENERAL WELFARE OF THE BLIND,

PELICAN BUILDINGS, PECKHAM ROAD, S.E.

Secretary . . . . . Mr. J. P. WILSON.

1. Number of Blind in the Town?
2. Objects of the Institution; if school, nature of Education?—To teach the Indigent Blind trades, and to find them employment.
3. When founded?—1857.
4. What system of Reading in use?
5. What number of male and female inmates, and amount charged (if any) for each?—None.
6. Age of admission, and how long they may remain?—No limit.
7. Qualification of Candidates for Admission?—Health and ability to work.
8. What Industrial occupations and trades are carried on—by males: and by females?—The manufacture of baskets, cutting firewood, brooms, brushes, mats, mattresses, and bedding.
9. Are outdoor pupils received for instruction in trades, and up to what age?—No.
10. How many Blind employed in the workshops?—30.
11. Blind or sighted teachers? Are sighted workmen employed to assist in finishing blind work, or as journeymen?—Sighted teachers. No.
12. Is there a retail shop?—Yes.
13. If so, are goods not made by the Blind sold in it?
14. What amount of goods were sold from the warehouse and retail shop last year, 1883?—1,065*l*.
15. When do the Managing Committee meet?—Weekly.
16. What were the subscriptions last year, 1883?—242*l*.
17. What were donations and legacies last year, 1883?—530*l*.
18. What income from endowments or trust funds?—None.
19. General remarks.—

PRESTON.

INDUSTRIAL INSTITUTE FOR THE BLIND,
GLOVER STREET, PRESTON.

Secretary . . THOMAS R. JOLLY.

1. Number of Blind in the Town?—About 150.
2. Objects of the Institution; if school, nature of Education?—To provide workshops for the Blind, and to teach ordinary branches of education, with music.
3. When founded?—1867.
4. What system of Reading in use?—Braille.
5. What number of male and female inmates, and amount charged (if any) for each?
6. Age of admission, and how long they may remain?
7. Qualification of Candidates for Admission?
8. What Industrial occupations and trades are carried on—by males: and by females?—Males: skip and basket making. Females: cane seating, knitting, &c.
9. Are pupils received for instruction in trades, and up to what age?—Yes; no limit to age.
10. How many Blind employed in the workshops?—21.
11. Blind or sighted teachers? Are sighted workmen employed to assist in finishing blind work, or as journeymen? Blind teachers.
12. Is there a retail shop?—Yes.
13. If so, are goods not made by the Blind sold in it?—Yes.
14. What amount of goods were sold from the warehouse and retail shop last year, 1883?—880*l*.
15. When do the Managing Committee meet?—The third Tuesday in each month.
16. What were the subscriptions last year, 1883?—154*l*.
17. What were donations and legacies last year, 1883?—142*l*.
18. What income from endowments or trust funds?—87*l*.
19. General remarks.—

PLYMOUTH.

SOUTH DEVON AND CORNWALL INSTITUTION FOR THE BLIND,

NORTH HILL, PLYMOUTH.

Honorary Secretary . . J. W. MATTHEWS, Esq.

1. Number of Blind in the Town ?—About 60.
2. Objects of the Institution; if school, nature of Education ?— To provide instruction in ordinary branches of education, with music for the Blind in a resident school; to teach them trades, and to provide employment for non-resident adult Blind.
3. When founded ?—1860.
4. What system of Reading in use ?—Lucas, Moon, and Braille.
5. What number of male and female inmates, and amount charged (if any) for each ?—35. 3s. to 5s. per week.
6. Age of admission, and how long they may remain ?—8 ; remain 3 and 5 years.
7. Qualification of Candidates for Admission ?
8. What Industrial occupations and trades are carried on—by males: and by females ?— Males: baskets and mats, matting and reed work. Females: knitting, wool work, and re-seating chairs.
9. Are outdoor pupils received for instruction in trades, and up to what age ?—Yes, up to 40 years.
10. How many Blind employed in the workshops ?—11.
11. Blind or sighted teachers ? Are sighted workmen employed to assist in finishing blind work, or as journeymen ?— Blind teachers. No.
12. Is there a retail shop ?—Yes.
13. If so, are goods not made by the Blind sold in it ?—No.
14. What amount of goods were sold from the warehouse and retail shop last year, 1883 ?—1,077*l*.
15. When do the Managing Committee meet ?—Second Tuesday in the month.
16. What were the subscriptions last year, 1883 ?—222*l*.
17. What were donations and legacies last year, 1883 ?—427*l*.
18. What income from endowments or trust funds ?—27*l*.
19. General remarks.—

SHEFFIELD.

SHEFFIELD INSTITUTION FOR THE BLIND,
WEST STREET, SHEFFIELD.
THE SCHOOL, MANCHESTER ROAD, SHEFFIELD.

Honorary Secretary . WILLIAM RAWSON CARTER, Esq.
Assistant Secretary . J. B. MEESON.

1. Number of Blind in the Town?—143.
2. Objects of the Institution; if school, nature of Education?—To provide a school for the education of the young Blind, and workshops for the adult Blind; also a visiting and benevolent association and lending library.
3. When founded?—1860.
4. What system of Reading in use?—Moon and Braille.
5. What number of male and female inmates, and amount charged (if any) for each?—24 boys and 21 girls in the school. Pupils are received at the school at the following charges, viz. if residing in Sheffield and under 12 years of age, 7*l.* per annum; if over 12 years, 10*l.* per annum. If from outside Sheffield and under 12 years, 10*l.* per annum; if over 12 years, 12*l.* per annum.
6. Age of admission, and how long they may remain?—7 years old and upwards; remain until considered sufficiently trained.
7. Qualification of Candidates for Admission?—Must be blind, or only just able to see light, and capable of receiving instruction.
8. What Industrial occupations and trades are carried on—by males: and by females?—Males: basket making, brush making, weaving, mat making. Females: brush making, chair caning, hassock making, sewing, knitting.
9. Are outdoor pupils received for instruction in trades, and up to what age?—Yes; at any age.
10. How many Blind employed in the workshops?—32.
11. Blind or sighted teachers? Are sighted workmen employed to assist in finishing blind work, or as journeymen?—Both.
12. Is there a retail shop?—Yes.
13. If so, are goods not made by the Blind sold in it?—Yes.
14. What amount of goods were sold from the warehouse and retail shop last year, 1883?—Over 2,000*l.*
15. When do the Managing Committee meet?—On Mondays.
16. What were the subscriptions last year, 1883?—170*l.*

17. What were donations and legacies last year, 1883?—38*l*.
18. What income from endowments or trust funds?—The school endowment from the late Mr. D. Holy's bequest is over 700*l*. per annum. The receipts from other trust funds were last year 208*l*.
19. General remarks.—Shoemaking has been tried at the school, but has not succeeded.

SOUTHSEA.

HAMPSHIRE AND ISLE OF WIGHT SCHOOL AND HOME FOR THE BLIND,

PARK LANE, SOUTHSEA.

Honorary Secretary . . Major-General WHITE.

1. Number of Blind in the Town?
2. Objects of the Institution; if school, nature of Education?—To provide instruction in ordinary branches of education, with music and singing, in a resident school, and instruction in trades and education, generally to enable the inmates to maintain themselves when leaving the school.
3. When founded?—1864.
4. What system of Reading in use?—Moon and Braille.
5. What number of male and female inmates, and amount charged (if any) for each?—6 boys, 11 girls; 10*l*. to 15*l*. per annum.
6. Age of admission, and how long they may remain?—Between 8 and 12.
7. Qualification of Candidates for Admission?—None.
8. What Industrial occupations and trades are carried on—by males: and by females?—Males: basket making, chair caning. Females: chair caning, knitting, netting.
9. Are outdoor pupils received for instruction in trades, and up to what age?—Yes; at any age.
10. How many Blind employed in the workshops?—7.
11. Blind or sighted teachers? Are sighted workmen employed to assist in finishing blind work, or as journeymen?—Blind teachers. Sighted, for education.
12. Is there a retail shop?—Yes.
13. If so, are goods not made by the Blind sold in it?—Yes.
14. What amount of goods were sold from the warehouse and retail shop last year, 1883?—448*l*.

INSTITUTIONS AND CHARITIES FOR THE BLIND.   49

15. When do the Managing Committee meet?—Every Friday.
16. What were the subscriptions last year, 1883?—151*l.*
17. What were donations and legacies last year, 1883?—61*l.*
18. What income from endowments or trust funds?—Nil.
19. General remarks.—The boys are drilled twice a week by a Sergeant of the Royal Marine Artillery.

*STOCKPORT.

INSTITUTE FOR THE BLIND, AND THE DEAF AND DUMB,

ST. PETER'S GATE.

Secretary . . . . Mr. N. CALVERT.

1. Number of Blind in the Town?
2. Objects of the Institution; if school, nature of Education?—To provide workshops for the Blind, and Deaf and Dumb, and to give instruction in reading to the Blind.
3. When founded?—1867.
4. What system of Reading in use?—Moon.
5. What number of male and female inmates, and amount charged (if any) for each?
6. Age of admission, and how long they may remain?
7. Qualification of Candidates for Admission?—Residence within three miles of Stockport; health and capacity. Total blindness not absolutely necessary.
8. What Industrial occupations and trades are carried on—by males: and by females?—Males: basket making, mat making, brush making. Females: chair caning, knitting.
9. Are outdoor pupils received for instruction in trades, and up to what age?—Yes, at any age.
10. How many Blind employed in the workshops?—18.
11. Blind or sighted teachers? Are sighted workmen employed to assist in finishing blind work, or as journeymen?
12. Is there a retail shop?—Yes: at the Institution.
13. If so, are goods not made by the Blind sold in it?
14. What amount of goods were sold from the warehouse and retail shop last year, 1883?—2,686*l.*
15. When do the Managing Committee meet?—Monthly.
16. What were the subscriptions last year, 1883?— ⎱ 176*l.*
17. What were donations and legacies last year, 1883?— ⎰
18. What income from endowments or trust funds?—85*l.*
19. General remarks.—

E

SUNDERLAND.

SUNDERLAND AND DURHAM COUNTY INSTITUTE FOR THE BLIND,

VILLIERS STREET, SUNDERLAND.

Honorary Secretary . . Miss BYERS.

1. Number of Blind in the Town?—About 100.
2. Objects of the Institution; if school, nature of Education?—To provide workshops for the Blind, and to provide for the education of the young Blind; also to teach the Blind to read at their homes.
3. When founded?—1877.
4. What system of Reading in use?—Moon and Braille.
5. What number of male and female inmates, and amount charged (if any) for each?—None.
6. Age of admission, and how long they may remain?
7. Qualification of Candidates for Admission?—Blindness.
8. What Industrial occupations and trades are carried on—by males: and by females?—Bed and mattress making, basket and mat making, and pianoforte tuning.
9. Are outdoor pupils received for instruction in trades, and up to what age?—Yes, at any age.
10. How many Blind employed in the workshops?—38.
11. Blind or sighted teachers? Are sighted workmen employed to assist in finishing blind work, or as journeymen?—Sighted teachers.
12. Is there a retail shop?—Yes.
13. If so, are goods not made by the Blind sold in it?—Yes.
14. What amount of goods were sold from the warehouse and retail shop last year, 1883?—5,550*l*.
15. When do the Managing Committee meet?—Once a week.
16. What were the subscriptions last year, 1883?— } 104*l*.
17. What were donations and legacies last year, 1883?—
18. What income from endowments or trust funds?—None.
19. General remarks.—The education of children has been handed over to School Board, who provide a Blind teacher and use a room at the Institution as a class-room.

SWANSEA.

SWANSEA AND SOUTH WALES INSTITUTION FOR THE BLIND,
SOUTH HILL PLACE, SWANSEA.

Honorary Secretary . . JOSEPH HALL, Esq.

1. Number of Blind in the Town?—70.
2. Objects of the Institution; if school, nature of Education?—To provide instruction in reading and music in a resident school, and to provide workshops, to teach trades, and give employment for the Blind.
3. When founded?—1865.
4. What system of Reading in use?—Moon and Braille.
5. What number of male and female inmates, and amount charged (if any) for each?—6 male, 8 female; 7s. per week under 14, 10s. over 14.
6. Age of admission, and how long they may remain?—9 and over; remain 3 to 5 years.
7. Qualification of Candidates for Admission? — Blindness; freedom from disease and vicious habit.
8. What Industrial occupations and trades are carried on—by males: and by females?—Males: basket making and mat making. Females: chair caning and knitting. Music to all.
9. Are outdoor pupils received for instruction in trades, and up to what age?—Yes; no restriction as to age.
10. How many Blind employed in the workshops?—18.
11. Blind or sighted teachers? Are sighted workmen employed to assist in finishing blind work, or as journeymen?—Sighted teachers.
12. Is there a retail shop?—Yes.
13. If so, are goods not made by the Blind sold in it?—Yes.
14. What amount of goods were sold from the warehouse and retail shop last year, 1883?—564*l*.
15. When do the Managing Committee meet?—Monthly.
16. What were the subscriptions last year, 1883?—247*l*.
17. What were donations and legacies last year, 1883?—58*l*.
18. What income from endowments or trust funds?
19. General remarks.—

WOLVERHAMPTON.

WOLVERHAMPTON SOCIETY FOR THE BLIND,
DARLINGTON STREET, WOLVERHAMPTON.

Honorary Secretary . . L. MAJOR, Esq.

1. Number of Blind in the Town?—136.
2. Objects of the Institution; if school, nature of Education?—To better the condition of the indigent outdoor Blind, and to teach them trades.
3. When founded?—1882.
4. What system of Reading in use?—Moon.
5. What number of male and female inmates, and amount charged (if any) for each?—8 males and 6 females.
6. Age of admission, and how long they may remain?—16 and upwards.
7. Qualification of Candidates for Admission?—Blindness and ability to work.
8. What Industrial occupations and trades are carried on—by males: and by females?—Males: basket making. Females: chair caning and knitting.
9. Are outdoor pupils received for instruction in trades, and up to what age?—Yes; any age.
10. How many Blind employed in the workshops?—14.
11. Blind or sighted teachers? Are sighted workmen employed to assist in finishing blind work, or as journeymen?—Sighted. No.
12. Is there a retail shop?—Yes.
13. If so, are goods not made by the Blind sold in it?—Yes.
14. What amount of goods were sold from the warehouse and retail shop last year, 1883?—124*l*.
15. When do the Managing Committee meet?—Monthly.
16. What were the subscriptions last year, 1883?—41*l*.
17. What were donations and legacies last year, 1883?—155*l*.
18. What income from endowments or trust funds?
19. General remarks.—

WORCESTER.

WORCESTER COLLEGE FOR THE BLIND SONS OF GENTLEMEN,

THE COMMANDERY, WORCESTER.

President and Visitor	The LORD BISHOP OF WORCESTER.
Head Master	Rev. S. FOSTER, M.A.
Second Master	G. LAMPMANN, Esq., B.A.

The College terms are three; commencing January 16, May 1, and September 5.

Pupils are received from 7 years of age, and are divided into juniors and seniors.

Seeing pupils are also received, the sons of clergymen being preferred, and a large reduction is made in their terms.

The aim is to give such an education as is obtained by seeing boys in public schools, and frequently the pupils take degrees at the Universities.

There are various scholarships given, varying from 20l. to 50l. per annum.

The charges are for education and board—

    Blind pupils: Juniors 80l. per annum.
                  Seniors 100l. ,, ,,
    Seeing pupils: Juniors 60l. ,, ,,
                  Seniors 80l. ,, ,,

The Head Master will afford all information.

YORK.

YORKSHIRE SCHOOL FOR THE BLIND,
YORK.

Honorary Secretary . . F. J. Munby, Esq.

1. Number of Blind in the Town?—143.
2. Objects of the Institution; if school, nature of Education?— To give blind pupils in a resident school such instruction as may enable them to obtain a livelihood, and instruction in ordinary branches of education.
3. When founded?—1833.
4. What system of Reading in use?—Moon, Roman, and Braille.
5. What number of male and female inmates, and amount charged (if any) for each?—42 males, 28 females. 10*l.* per year.
6. Age of admission, and how long they may remain?—From 10 to 16; until 20 years of age.
7. Qualification of Candidates for Admission?—Sufficient intellect and health to be able to be taught.
8. What Industrial occupations and trades are carried on—by males: and by females?—Males: basket making, brush making, music, including tuning. Females: wool work, crochet, reseating chairs in cane.
9. Are outdoor pupils received for instruction in trades, and up to what age?—Yes.
10. How many Blind employed in the workshops?—31.
11. Blind or sighted teachers? Are sighted workmen employed to assist in finishing blind work, or as journeymen? Both. Sighted workmen employed in both ways.
12. Is there a retail shop?—Yes, at the Institution.
13. If so, are goods not made by the Blind sold in it?—Yes.
14. What amount of goods were sold from the warehouse and retail shop last year, 1883?—2,236*l.*
15. When do the Managing Committee meet?—Second Friday in each month.
16. What were the subscriptions last year, 1883?—414*l.*
17. What were donations and legacies last year, 1883?—1,610*l.*
18. What income from endowments or trust funds? 1,235*l.*
19. General remarks.

List of Charities for the Blind in the United Kingdom.

	PAGE
Bristol	56
Dublin	56
Dublin	57
Essex	57
Hastings	58
Ipswich	58
Limerick	59
Lanark	59
Gardner's Trust, London	60
Clothworkers' Co., Acton, London	61
Clothworkers' Co., Cornell, London	61
Clothworkers' Co., Gregory, London	62
Clothworkers' Co., Love, London	62
Clothworkers' Co., Newman, London	63
Clothworkers' Co., Thwaytes, London	63
Clothworkers' Co., West, London	64
Goldsmiths' Co., Farmer, London	64
Goldsmiths' Co., Cureton, London	65
Cordwainers' Co., Came, London	65
Day, London	66
Hetherington, London	67
Drapers' Co., Granger, London	68
Hunston, London	68
Painter Stainers', London	69
Protestant Blind Pension, London	70
British and Foreign Association, London	70
St. George's Fields, Annuities, London	71
Jews' Society, London	71
Governesses', London	72
Home for Aged Christian Women, London	72
East London Home, London	73
Female Annuity, London	73
Christian Relief Society, London	74
Hon. Frances Harley Charity, London	74
Somers Town Aid Society, London	75
South London Association, London	75
Indigent Blind Visiting, London	76
Girdlers' Co., London	76
Alma Street Home, London	76
Marlborough Street Society, London	76
Society for Prevention of Blindness, London	76
York Emmanuel	77

BRISTOL.

HOME FOR BLIND WOMEN,
25 ST. MICHAEL'S HILL, BRISTOL.

Honorary Secretary . . Miss CAROLINE BUSH.

1. Object of Charity?—To provide a permanent home for blind women aged 20 and upwards.
2. When founded?—1874.
3. Number of Blind being benefited?—11.
4. Number of Applications on Books?
5. Qualifications of Candidates?
6. When do the Managing Committee meet?—Quarterly.
7. When Elections take place?
8. Subscriptions received last year, 1883?— ⎫
9. Donations and Legacies received last year?— ⎬ 325*l*.
10. Income from Endowment?
11. General Remarks.—The inmates knit and cane chairs; and Moon's type is used.

DUBLIN.

*ST. MARY'S CATHOLIC HOME FOR FEMALES,
MERRION, DUBLIN

Secretary . . J. GREENE, Esq.

1. Object of Charity?—To receive Roman Catholic girls and women into a Conventual Institution and give them instruction.
2. When founded?—1863.
3. Number of Blind being benefited?
4. Number of Applications on Books?
5. Qualifications of Candidates?
6. When do the Managing Committee meet?
7. When Elections take place?
8. Subscriptions received last year, 1883?
9. Donations and Legacies received last year?
10. Income from Endowment?
11. General Remarks.—In another Conventual Institution at Glasnevin, blind men and boys are received in the same way.

DUBLIN.

SIMPSON'S HOSPITAL FOR THE BLIND AND GOUTY.

Secretary . . Jas. Young, Esq.

---

1. Object of Charity?—To provide a home for blind and gouty men, who have once been respectable merchants, traders, or professional men in Ireland.
2. When founded?—1779.
3. Number of Blind being benefited?—56 to 66.
4. Number of Applications on Books?
5. Qualifications of Candidates?—Good character, and having been in respectable circumstances.
6. When do the Managing Committee meet?—First Monday in February, May, August, and November.
7. When Elections take place?—First Monday in May and November.
8. Subscriptions received last year, 1883?—*Nil.*
9. Donations and Legacies received last year?—£300.
10. Income from Endowment?—*Nil.*
11. General Remarks.—The Institution is supported by rents of land and houses, which of late years have varied considerably. Applications must be lodged a month before the first Monday in May or November.

ESSEX.

DAME RASHDALE'S CHARITY FOR THE BLIND.

Trustees: { Thos. Chalk Swinborne, Thos. Simpson, } Coggeshall, Essex.

---

1. Object of Charity?—Relief of six blind women.
2. When founded?
3. Number of Blind being benefited?—Six.
4. Number of Applications on Books?—None.
5. Qualifications of Candidates?—Poverty and respectability.
6. When do the Managing Committee meet?—There is none.
7. When Elections take place?—None.
8. Subscriptions received last year, 1883?—None.
9. Donations and Legacies received last year?—None.
10. Income from Endowment?—30*l.* a year.
11. General Remarks.—Relief is given irrespective of place, or religious or political opinions.

HASTINGS.

SOCIETY FOR THE BENEFIT OF THE BLIND,
47 MAGDALEN STREET, ST. LEONARD'S-ON-SEA.

Honorary Secretary . . Miss MARSH.

1. Object of Charity?—To grant relief to aged or infirm blind persons of the neighbourhood.
2. When founded?
3. Number of Blind being benefited?—Three.
4. Number of Applications on Books?
5. Qualifications of Candidates?
6. When do the Managing Committee meet?
7. When Elections take place?
8. Subscriptions received last year, 1883?—83*l.*
9. Donations and Legacies received last year?—25*l.*
10. Income from Endowment?—3*l.*
11. General Remarks.—

IPSWICH.

IPSWICH AND SUFFOLK INSTITUTION FOR THE BLIND.

Secretary . . Vacant.

1. Object of Charity?—To ameliorate the condition of the Blind in Suffolk.
2. When founded?
3. Number of Blind being benefited?—3.
4. Number of Applications on Books?
5. Qualifications of Candidates?
6. When do the Managing Committee meet?
7. When Elections take place?
8. Subscriptions received last year, 1883?
9. Donations and Legacies received?—In 1882, 67*l.*
10. Income from Endowment?—51*l.*
11. General Remarks.—Three pupils are sent to the Asylum for the Blind at Norwich.

LIMERICK.

THE ASYLUM FOR BLIND FEMALES,
CATHERINE STREET, LIMERICK.

Secretary . . Rev. Canon GREGG, M.A.

1. Object of Charity?—To provide a Protestant Home for blind females of good character.
2. When founded?—1834.
3. Number of Blind being benefited?—12.
4. Number of Applications on Books?—None.
5. Qualifications of Candidates?—Good character. Preference to natives of County Limerick.
6. When do the Managing Committee meet?—When required.
7. When Elections take place?
8. Subscriptions received last year, 1883?— } 487*l.*
9. Donations and Legacies received last year?—
10. Income from Endowment?—107*l.*
11. General Remarks.—This is simply a domestic home for Protestant blind women; the inmates are described as being a 'united, happy Christian family.' It is connected with Trinity Church adjoining, where one of the inmates acts as organist.

LANARK, N.B.

SMYLLUM ORPHANAGE,
SMYLLUM PARK, LANARK.

Secretary . . Sister TERESA FARRELL.

1. Object of Charity?—The religious and secular instruction of Roman Catholic blind children in Scotland.
2. When founded?—1874.
3. Number of Blind being benefited?—6.
4. Number of Applications on Books?
5. Qualifications of Candidates?—Nothing but blindness.
6. When do the Managing Committee meet?
7. When Elections take place?
8. Subscriptions received last year, 1883?
9. Donations and Legacies received last year?
10. Income from Endowment?

11. General Remarks.—This really is an Orphanage, to which blind children are admitted, and is supported by the parochial Board, and by Government grants and charitable contributions.

LONDON.

GARDNER'S TRUST FOR THE BLIND,

1 POET'S CORNER, WESTMINSTER, LONDON, S.W.

Secretary . . . HENRY J. WILSON, Esq.

1. Object of Charity?—To provide instruction in music, in suitable trades, handicrafts, and professions; to provide pensions, and generally to assist the Blind as the Committee think best.
2. When founded?—1879.
3. Number of Blind being benefited?—395 persons. 39 Institutions for the Blind.
4. Number of Applications on Books?—Nearly 3,000.
5. Qualifications of Candidates?—For pensions applicants must be of good moral character, and not in receipt of parish relief. For scholarships applicants must be between 7 and 25 years of age, according to the conditions under which the scholarships are founded. In all cases no restriction as to religious opinions, and all must be residents in England or Wales.
6. When do the Managing Committee meet?—First Tuesday in the month.
7. When Elections take place?—When vacancies occur.
8. Subscriptions received last year, 1883?
9. Donations and Legacies received last year?—*Nil.*
10. Income from Endowment?—Interest on 300,000*l.*
11. General Remarks.—Applicants should send full particulars as to name, age, and income. The pensions vary from 10*l.* to 20*l.* per annum. Scholarships have been founded at various Institutions; leave to compete must be applied for to the Secretary.

LONDON.

CLOTHWORKERS' CHARITIES FOR THE BLIND.

See under Acton, Cornell, Gregory, Love, Newman, Thwaytes, and West.

ACTON'S CHARITY FOR THE BLIND,
CLOTHWORKERS' HALL, 41 MINCING LANE, LONDON, E.C.

Secretary . . O. ROBERTS, Esq., M.A.

1. Object of Charity?—To grant pensions of 10*l*.
2. When founded?—1837.
3. Number of Blind being benefited?—4.
4. Number of Applications on Books?
5. Qualifications of Candidates?—Applicants must be 50 years of age, of sober life and good morals, have been totally blind for 3 years, not be entitled to any estate, annuity, salary, pension, or income to the amount of 20*l*. a year; nor be an inmate of a workhouse or public institution; nor publicly solicit nor receive alms.
6. When do the Managing Committee meet?
7. When Elections take place?—When vacancies occur.
8. Subscriptions received last year, 1883?
9. Donations and Legacies received last year?
10. Income from Endowment?—32*l*.
11. General Remarks.—Blank petitions are issued from the Company's office between the hours of 11 and 3. Certificates of age, blindness, circumstances, and marriage (if married) must be annexed to the petition. The petition, the certificate, or declaration of age, the certificate of the surgeon, and the certificate of facts, properly filled up and signed, are to be delivered gratis at the Company's office at the Company's Hall, Mincing Lane, London.

CORNELL'S CHARITY FOR THE BLIND,
CLOTHWORKERS' HALL, 41 MINCING LANE, LONDON, E.C.

Secretary . . O. ROBERTS, Esq., M.A.

1. Object of Charity?—To grant pensions of 10*l*.
2. When founded?—1850.
3. Number of Blind being benefited?—6.
4. Number of Applications on Books?
5. Qualifications of Candidates?—Must be citizens of London; and as Acton's Charity.

LONDON.

6. When do the Managing Committee meet?
7. When Elections take place?
8. Subscriptions received last year, 1883?
9. Donations and Legacies received last year?
10. Income from Endowment?—70*l.*
11. General Remarks.—

GREGORY'S CHARITY FOR THE BLIND,
CLOTHWORKERS' HALL, 41 MINCING LANE, LONDON, E.C.

Secretary . . O. ROBERTS, Esq., M.A.

---

1. Object of Charity?—To grant a pension of 4*l.* per annum.
2. When founded?—1845.
3. Number of Blind being benefited?—One.
4. Number of Applications on Books?
5. Qualifications of Candidates?—One of the two most aged Blind pensioners of Clothworkers' Company; and as Acton's Charity.
6. When do the Managing Committee meet?
7. When Elections take place?
8. Subscriptions received last year, 1883?
9. Donations and Legacies received last year?
10. Income from Endowment?—4*l.*
11. General Remarks.—

LOVE'S CHARITY FOR THE BLIND,
CLOTHWORKERS' HALL, 41 MINCING LANE, LONDON, E.C.

Secretary . . O. ROBERTS, Esq., M.A.

---

1. Object of Charity?—To grant a pension of 10*l.* per annum.
2. When founded?—1858.
3. Number of Blind being benefited?—One.
4. Number of Applications on Books?
5. Qualifications of Candidates?—50 years of age, and 3 years blind; and as Acton's Charity.
6. When do the Managing Committee meet?
7. When Elections take place?
8. Subscriptions received last year, 1883?—*Nil.*
9. Donations and Legacies received last year?—*Nil.*
10. Income from Endowment?—8*l.* 1*s.* 6*d.*
11. General Remarks.—

LONDON.

NEWMAN'S CHARITY FOR THE BLIND,

CLOTHWORKERS' HALL, 41 MINCING LANE, LONDON, E.C.

Secretary . . O. ROBERTS, Esq., M.A.

1. Object of Charity?—To grant pensions of 10l. per annum.
2. When founded?—1810.
3. Number of Blind being benefited?—32.
4. Number of Applications on Books?
5. Qualifications of Candidates?—50 years of age, 3 years blind; and as Acton's Charity.
6. When do the Managing Committee meet?—May and November.
7. When Elections take place?
8. Subscriptions received last year, 1883?
9. Donations and Legacies received last year?
10. Income from Endowment?—382l. 10s.
11. General Remarks.—

THWAYTES'S CHARITY FOR THE BLIND,

CLOTHWORKERS' HALL, 41 MINCING LANE, LONDON, E.C.

Secretary . . O. ROBERTS, Esq., M.A.

1. Object of Charity?—To grant pensions of 10l. per annum.
2. When founded?—1835.
3. Number of Blind being benefited?—100.
4. Number of Applications on Books?
5. Qualifications of Candidates?—50 years old, 3 years blind; and as Acton's Charity.
6. When do the Managing Committee meet?—May and November.
7. When Elections take place?—When vacancies occur.
8. Subscriptions received last year, 1883?
9. Donations and Legacies received last year?
10. Income from Endowment?—671l.
11. General Remarks.—

LONDON.

WEST'S CHARITY FOR THE BLIND,
CLOTHWORKERS' HALL, 41 MINCING LANE, LONDON, E.C.

Secretary . . O. ROBERTS, Esq., M.A.

1. Object of Charity?—To grant pensions of 5*l*. per annum.
2. When founded?—1718.
3. Number of Blind being benefited?—487.
4. Number of Applications on Books?
5. Qualifications of Candidates?—50 years old, 3 years blind; preference to West's kin and natives of Newbury, Reading, Twickenham, Isleworth, Richmond, City of London, and Henley-on-Thames. Further, as Acton's Charity.
6. When do the Managing Committee meet?—June and December.
7. When Elections take place?
8. Subscriptions received last year, 1883?
9. Donations and Legacies received last year?
10. Income from Endowment?
11. General Remarks.—

FARMER'S CHARITY FOR THE BLIND,
GOLDSMITHS' HALL, ST. MARTIN'S-LE-GRAND, LONDON, E.C.

Secretary . . W. S. PRIDEAUX, Esq.

1. Object of Charity?—To grant pensions of 4*l*. per annum.
2. When founded?—1813.
3. Number of Blind being benefited?—10.
4. Number of Applications on Books?
5. Qualifications of Candidates?—None.
6. When do the Managing Committee meet?
7. When Elections take place?
8. Subscriptions received last year, 1883?
9. Donations and Legacies received last year?
10. Income from Endowment?
11. General Remarks.—1. Preference is given to Freemen of Goldsmiths' Company who are of the craft. 2. To other Freemen of the Company, and their widows. 3. To Freemen of the City of London, and their widows.

LONDON.

CURETON'S CHARITY FOR THE BLIND,
GOLDSMITHS' HALL, ST. MARTIN'S-LE-GRAND, LONDON, E.C.

Secretary . . W. S. PRIDEAUX, Esq.

1. Object of Charity?—To grant pensions of 20*l.* per annum.
2. When founded?—1858.
3. Number of Blind being benefited?—5.
4. Number of Applications on Books?
5. Qualifications of Candidates?—50 years of age; totally blind for 12 months; income not exceeding 25*l.* per annum; receiving nothing from other Charity on account of blindness.
6. When do the Managing Committee meet?
7. When Elections take place?
8. Subscriptions received last year, 1883?
9. Donations and Legacies received last year?
10. Income from Endowment?
11. General Remarks.—Preference is given as in Farmer's Charity.

CAME'S CHARITY FOR THE BLIND,
CORDWAINERS' HALL, 7 CANNON STREET, LONDON, E.C.

Secretary . . H. JACKSON, Esq.

1. Object of Charity?—To give pensions of 5*l.* per annum.
2. When founded?—1796.
3. Number of Blind being benefited?—115.
4. Number of Applications on Books?—30.
5. Qualifications of Candidates?—Total blindness; residence within 100 miles of London; never to have begged in the streets, or received relief from parish. Men must be 46; married women, 40; widows and maids, 30.
6. When do the Managing Committee meet?—November.
7. When Elections take place?—December.

LONDON.

8. Subscriptions received last year, 1883?
9. Donations and Legacies received last year?
10. Income from Endowment?—About 575*l*.
11. General Remarks.—The application must be made before the 10th of November, by petition to the Master, Wardens, and Court of Assistants of the Company, stating means of support, age (proved by certificate or declaration), and any special circumstances, verified by the signatures of six of the principal inhabitants of the parish in which the petitioner is living at the date of the petition; if petitioner is married, a marriage certificate must be produced. The petition of a successful candidate must be renewed at the end of three years.

DAY'S CHARITY FOR THE BLIND,

34 SAVILE ROW, LONDON, W.

Secretary . . PINDER SIMPSON, Esq.

---

1. Object of Charity?—To give pensions of 12*l.*, 16*l.*, or 20*l.* per annum to deserving Blind.
2. When founded?—1836.
3. Number of Blind being benefited?—237.
4. Number of Applications on Books?—3,000.
5. Qualifications of Candidates?—Wholly blind; proper object for relief; resident in England, Wales, or Scotland.
6. When do the Managing Committee meet?—Quarterly.
7. When Elections take place?—January, April, July, October.
8. Subscriptions received last year, 1883?
9. Donations and Legacies received last year?
10. Income from Endowment?—3,653*l*.
11. General Remarks.—The trustees who elect Pensioners are (1884) W. Underwood, Esq., J. Shaw, Esq., and E. C. Johnson, Esq.

LONDON.

HETHERINGTON'S CHARITY FOR THE AGED BLIND,

CHRIST'S HOSPITAL, NEWGATE STREET, LONDON, E.C.

Clerk . . M. S. S. DIPNALL, Esq.

---

1. Object of Charity?—To provide annuities of 10*l*. to aged blind persons who 'have seen better days.'
2. When founded?—1774.
3. Number of Blind being benefited?—706.
4. Number of Applications on Books?—250 annually.
5. Qualifications of Candidates?[1]—Age, 61 years or upwards. Birth and residence in England, to the exclusion of Wales and Berwick-upon-Tweed. Total blindness for three whole years, and *residence during that period* at the place where the blind person resides at the time of petitioning. Income, if any, under 20*l*. a year.
6. When do the Managing Committee meet?— } In November
7. When Elections take place?— } and February.
8. Subscriptions received last year, 1883?
9. Donations and Legacies received last year?
10. Income from Endowment?—7,672*l*., subject to certain payments to Christ's Hospital for management, &c.
11.—General Remarks.—Forms of petition may be had on application at the Counting-house, Christ's Hospital, in the month of October only. Prospectuses of the Charity may be had on application at any time. Petitions of unsuccessful candidates are to be renewed annually. About 100 are elected annually.

---

[1] The intention of the Founder of the above-mentioned Charity (as expressed by himself) was to relieve such persons only as, *having been in a better situation of life*, are or may be disabled by blindness from maintaining themselves, and on that account are or may become a burden upon their children or relations, not in affluent circumstances; or, having but little of their own, want some addition to what they have to make life more comfortable under such an infirmity. The Governors, therefore, to prevent disappointment to many otherwise deserving applicants, give notice that persons of the following descriptions are deemed ineligible to the Charity, viz.:—

Day labourers of every denomination,—common soldiers, and sailors,—militia men, unless principals serving for themselves,—domestic and menial servants of gentlemen,—journeymen in any handicraft trade, persons living by turning a mangle, a polisher's wheel, or other like employment; and also those who have ever begged, *or have at any time during their lives received any parochial alms or allowance as paupers*.

LONDON.

GRANGER'S CHARITY FOR THE BLIND,
DRAPERS' HALL, 27 THROGMORTON STREET, LONDON, E.C.

Clerk . . W. P. SAWYER, Esq.

1. Object of Charity?—To grant pensions of 10l. to indigent blind persons every second year.
2. When founded?—1835.
3. Number of Blind being benefited?—14.
4. Number of Applications on Books?
5. Qualifications of Candidates?—The Court of Wardens elect from candidates who present a certificate of 'good fame for honesty and sobriety' from ministers and churchwardens of their parish.
6. When do the Managing Committee meet?
7. When Elections take place?
8. Subscriptions received last year, 1883?
9. Donations and Legacies received last year?
10. Income from Endowment?
11. General Remarks.—

HUNSTON'S CHARITY FOR THE BLIND,
*THE VESTRY OF ST. BOTOLPH, ALDGATE, LONDON, E.C.

Secretary . . . CLERK OF THE VESTRY.

1. Object of Charity?—To grant pensions of 12l. to indigent Blind, originally of the parishes of St. Botolph, Aldgate, St. John, Wapping, and St. Paul's, Shadwell.
2. When founded?—1777.
3. Number of Blind being benefited?—4.
4. Number of Applications on Books?
5. Qualifications of Candidates?—Preference given to lightermen, their widows and children.
6. When do the Managing Committee meet?
7. When Elections take place?
8. Subscriptions received last year, 1883?
9. Donations and Legacies received last year?
10. Income from Endowment?—About 59l.
11. General Remarks.—Applications to the Clerk of the Vestry, St. Botolph.

LONDON.

PAINTER STAINERS' CHARITIES FOR THE BLIND,

PAINTER STAINERS' HALL, 9 LITTLE TRINITY LANE, LONDON, E.C.

Secretaries . . { H. D. PRITCHARD, Esq.
{ W. TENGLEFIELD, Esq.

---

1. Object of Charity?—To give pensions of 10*l.* each to blind persons, granted under the wills of John Stock, Esq., 1780; Mrs. Dorothy Smith, 1790; Mrs. Jane Shank, 1795; Mrs. Mary Grainger, 1808; Mrs. Ann Yeates, 1794; and Miss Ann Rhodes Syddall, 1861.
2. When founded?—About 1800.
3. Number of Blind being benefited?—174.
4. Number of Applications on Books?
5. Qualifications of Candidates?—[1] 61 years of age complete. Have been totally blind for three years. Unable to maintain themselves. In distressed circumstances. Born in England, not in Wales or Scotland. Must have lived three years in their present parish or place of residence. Have no income for life above 10*l.* a year, nor receiving any benefaction to that amount. Have never received alms from any parish or place as a pauper. Never been a common beggar. Of sober life and conversation.
6. When do the Managing Committee meet?
7. When Elections take place?—Second Wednesday in December.
8. Subscriptions received last year, 1883?
9. Donations and Legacies received last year?
10. Income from Endowment?
11. General Remarks.—A blank form of petition containing all requisite information is supplied direct to applicants from October 25 to November 30 every year. Unsuccessful petitioners may apply a second time.

---

[1] These being the qualifications prescribed by the Benefactors and Donors of the Charities, the Trustees cannot depart from them in the slightest degree; and they must be testified to by the Minister and the Churchwardens of the parish in which the petitioner resides. The petitioner must also furnish certificates of baptism; if married, of marriage, and of *total* blindness from a Surgeon.

LONDON.

PROTESTANT BLIND PENSION SOCIETY,
235 SOUTHWARK BRIDGE ROAD, LONDON, S.E.

Secretary . . Mr. W. Elliott Terry.

1. Object of Charity?—To grant pensions commencing at 10s. per month to indigent blind persons of any denomination.
2. When founded?—1863.
3. Number of Blind being benefited?—425.
4. Number of Applications on Books?—198.
5. Qualifications of Candidates?—Blindness and poverty.
6. When do the Managing Committee meet?—Monthly.
7. When Elections take place?—Half-yearly.
8. Subscriptions received last year, 1883?—1,630l.
9. Donations and Legacies received last year?—1,342l.
10. Income from Endowment?—Nil.
11. General Remarks.—

BRITISH AND FOREIGN BLIND ASSOCIATION,
33 CAMBRIDGE SQUARE, LONDON, W.

Honorary Secretary . . T. R. Armitage, Esq., M.D.

1. Object of Charity?—To discover the best methods of educating and employing the Blind, and to obtain their general adoption; also to produce school apparatus, books, music, maps, &c.
2. When founded?—1868.
3. Number of Blind being benefited?
4. Number of Applications on Books?
5. Qualifications of Candidates?
6. When do the Managing Committee meet?—First Wednesday in the month.
7. When Elections take place?
8. Subscriptions received last year, 1883?—91l.
9. Donations and Legacies received last year?—153l.
10. Income from Endowment?—Nil.
11. General Remarks.—The Executive Council consists of blind gentlemen. Two males are employed stereotyping; 1 carpenter; and about 40 males and females writing MS. books in Braille type. See also 'Notice of Books in Braille Type' issued by this Society, p. 91.

LONDON.

SOCIETY FOR GRANTING ANNUITIES TO THE POOR ADULT BLIND,

BLIND SCHOOL, ST. GEORGE'S FIELDS, LONDON, S.E.

Secretary . . Rev. B. G. JOHNS.

1. Object of Charity?—To aid in the support of poor blind persons of good character, who, being by age ineligible for admission into schools, unable to do industrial work, and unwilling to beg, have no sufficient means of support.
2. When founded?—1859.
3. Number of Blind being benefited?—36.
4. Number of Applications on Books?—50.
5. Qualifications of Candidates?—Not under 40. Good character. Income not exceeding 10l. per annum.
6. When do the Managing Committee meet?
7. When Elections take place?—Generally in May.
8. Subscriptions received last year, 1883?—160l.
9. Donations and Legacies received last year?—Nil.
10. Income from Endowment?—Nil.
11. General Remarks.—

*JEWS' SOCIETY FOR THE RELIEF OF INDIGENT BLIND JEWS,

5 DUKE STREET, ALDGATE, LONDON, E.C.

Secretary . . Mr. S. SOLOMON.

1. Object of Charity?—To give 8s. per week to indigent blind Jews for life.
2. When founded?—1819.
3. Number of Blind being benefited?—54.
4. Number of Applications on Books?
5. Qualifications of Candidates?—A petition signed by three governors, and certificate of surgeon as to total blindness. Residence in England for five years. No relief from other Institution.
6. When do the Managing Committee meet?
7. When Elections take place?—Usually in July.
8. Subscriptions received last year, 1883?— ⎫
9. Donations and Legacies received last year?— ⎬ 1,100l.
10. Income from Endowment?— ⎭
11. General Remarks.—Petitions must be left with the Secretary, within 14 days of notice of vacancy.

LONDON.

'GOVERNESSES' BENEVOLENT INSTITUTION FOR THE BLIND,
32 SACKVILLE STREET, LONDON, W.

Secretary . . W. C. KLUGH, Esq.

1. Object of Charity?—To give pensions to blind governesses.
2. When founded?—1860.
3. Number of Blind being benefited?—7.
4. Number of Applications on Books?
5. Qualifications of Candidates?—Must have been governesses, not including keepers of, or teachers in, schools. Above 50 years of age. Single or widows. Candidates must be approved by the Board before election.
6. When do the Managing Committee meet?
7. When Elections take place?
8. Subscriptions received last year, 1883?
9. Donations and Legacies received last year?
10. Income from Endowment?—174*l*.
11. General Remarks.—Marriage vacates the annuity; and it is also vacated by any transfer of any kind.

HOME FOR AGED CHRISTIAN BLIND WOMEN,
MANSION HOUSE, HANLEY ROAD, LONDON, N.

Secretary . . Rev. J. R. WOOD.

1. Object of Charity?—To provide a Home for aged blind Christian women over 50.
2. When founded?—1880.
3. Number of Blind being benefited?—24.
4. Number of Applications on Books?
5. Qualifications of Candidates?—Over 50 years old. Poverty, blindness, piety.
6. When do the Managing Committee meet?—Last Thursday in the month.
7. When Elections take place?—No elections.
8. Subscriptions received last year, 1883?— } 667*l*.
9. Donations and Legacies received last year?—
10. Income from Endowment?
11. General Remarks.—Each inmate in receipt of a pension, or income, is expected to pay part of maintenance. A limited number of paying visitors are taken at 12*s*. 6*d*. per week.

INSTITUTIONS AND CHARITIES FOR THE BLIND. 73

LONDON.

EAST LONDON HOME AND SCHOOL FOR BLIND CHILDREN,

NELSON HOUSE, COLLEGE AVENUE, HACKNEY, E.

Secretary . . Miss RYE.

1. Object of Charity?—To educate and train blind children in Industrial occupations from 2 years of age to 14.
2. When founded?—1874.
3. Number of Blind being benefited?—14.
4. Number of Applications on Books?
5. Qualifications of Candidates?—Total or partial blindness.
6. When do the Managing Committee meet?
7. When Elections take place?
8. Subscriptions received last year, 1883?—422l.
9. Donations and Legacies received last year?
10. Income from Endowment?
11. General Remarks.—This Home is the only Institution which receives blind children so young.

BLIND FEMALE ANNUITY SOCIETY,

25 FAIRFAX ROAD, SOUTH HAMPSTEAD, N.W.

Secretary . . Miss DANVERS.

1. Object of Charity?—To assist respectable blind women, being either widows or spinsters.
2. When founded?—1875.
3. Number of Blind being benefited?—17.
4. Number of Applications on Books?
5. Qualifications of Candidates?
6. When do the Managing Committee meet?—Once a quarter.
7. When Elections take place?
8. Subscriptions received last year, 1883?—89l.
9. Donations and Legacies received last year?—334l.
10. Income from Endowment?—20l.
11. General Remarks.—

LONDON.

CHRISTIAN BLIND RELIEF SOCIETY,
59 BURDETT ROAD, BOW, LONDON, E.

Secretary . . T. CLARKE, Esq.

1. Object of Charity?—To grant pensions to needy and deserving Blind of good moral character in all parts of the United Kingdom, irrespective of any religious qualification.
2. When founded?
3. Number of Blind being benefited?—140.
4. Number of Applications on Books?
5. Qualifications of Candidates?—Poverty. Income must not exceed 20*l*. if single, 30*l*. if married. Recommendation of annual subscriber of 1*l*. 1*s*., or donor of 10*l*. 10*s*. necessary.
6. When do the Managing Committee meet?
7. When Elections take place?
8. Subscriptions received last year, 1883?— } 473*l*.
9. Donations and Legacies received last year?—
10. Income from Endowment?
11. General Remarks.—

HON. MISS FRANCES HARLEY'S CHARITIES FOR THE BLIND.

Solicitors to Trustees . Messrs. C. and S. HARRISON & Co.,
19 Bedford Row, London, W.C.

1. Object of Charity?—To help to maintain four blind persons and widows of clergymen of the Church of England and Ireland.
2. When founded?
3. Number of Blind being benefited?—24.
4. Number of Applications on Books?—60.
5. Qualifications of Candidates?—For poor Blind: Membership of the Church of England and Ireland. For Clergymen's Widows Fund: Must be widow of a clergyman who should have resided, and had cure, within the Counties of Hereford, Brecon, and Radnor, and must be in reduced circumstances.
6. When do the Managing Committee meet?—No certain time.
7. When Elections take place?—When vacancies occur.
8. Subscriptions received last year, 1883?

LONDON.

9. Donations and Legacies received last year?
10. Income from Endowment?—639*l*.
11. General Remarks.—Each applicant must produce some friends with whom it is proposed that the applicant shall reside.

SOMERS TOWN BLIND AID SOCIETY,

53 HILLDROP ROAD, LONDON, N.

Secretary . . Miss JESSIE HEPBURN STAREY.

---

1. Object of Charity?—To aid the temporal and spiritual welfare of the poor Blind of London.
2. When founded?—1864.
3. Number of Blind being benefited?—About 150.
4. Number of Applications on Books?—14.
5. Qualifications of Candidates?—Blindness, good character, and poverty.
6. When do the Managing Committee meet?—Quarterly.
7. When Elections take place?—Quarterly.
8. Subscriptions received last year, 1883?— } 510*l*.
9. Donations and Legacies received last year?—
10. Income from Endowment?
11. General Remarks.—The Society provides recreation, home teaching, small pensions, medical aid, &c., for the Blind.

SOUTH LONDON ASSOCIATION FOR ASSISTING THE BLIND,

15 BRIXTON ROAD, S.W.

Secretary . . J. T. EDMONDS, Esq.

---

1. Object of Charity?—Principally to teach the Blind to read; but it also assists the Blind with loans, finds employment for them when possible, and visits the sick.
2. When founded?—1863.
3. Number of Blind being benefited?—110.
4. Number of Applications on Books?
5. Qualifications of Candidates?—Recommendation of Subscribers.

LONDON.

6. When do the Managing Committee meet?
7. When Elections take place?
8. Subscriptions received, 1882?
9. Donations and Legacies received, 1882? } 480*l*.
10. Income from Endowment?
11. General Remarks.—

THE INDIGENT BLIND VISITING SOCIETY,
27 RED LION SQUARE, LONDON, W.C.

Secretary . . . Mr. W. C. LESTER.

---

1. Object of Charity?—To improve the condition of the Blind in and near London.
2. When founded?—1834.
3. Number of Blind being benefited?
4. Number of Applications on Books?
5. Qualifications of Candidates?
6. When do the Managing Committee meet?—Monthly.
7. When Elections take place?
8. Subscriptions received last year, 1883?—880*l*.
9. Donations and Legacies received last year?—1,809*l*.
10. Income from Endowment?—928*l*.
11. General Remarks.—

The Girdlers' Company, 59 Basinghall Street, E.C., administer PALYN'S CHARITY FOR THE POOR, resident in London, who are unable by infirmity to support themselves. Blindness gives a claim. The Clerk is J. E. PHILBRICK, Esq.

There is a small Home for the Blind at 44 Alma Street, London, N.W. Honorary Secretary, Miss Gill.

There is an Association for Improving the Condition of the Blind, in connection with Lending Library and Reading-rooms, at 53 Marlborough Street, London; of which the Misses Perry are Honorary Secretaries.

There is a Society for the Prevention of Blindness, and Improvement of the Physique of the Blind, of which the Honorary Secretary (*pro tem.*) is Dr. Roth, 48 Wimpole Street, London, W.

YORK.

THE YORK EMMANUEL,

18 LENDAL, YORK.

Secretary . . F. W. CALVERT, Esq.

1. Object of Charity?—To benefit ministers, and wives, or widows and children of ministers of this kingdom, who are blind or idiotic.
2. When founded?—1781.
3. Number of Blind being benefited?
4. Number of Applications on Books?—2 or 3.
5. Qualifications of Candidates?—Candidates' applications must be authenticated by one Justice of the Peace and two Ministers of the neighbourhood, together with medical certificate.
6. When do the Managing Committee meet?—Half-yearly.
7. When Elections take place?—At each meeting.
8. Subscriptions received last year, 1883?—*Nil.*
9. Donations and Legacies received last year?—*Nil.*
10. Income from Endowment?—500*l.*
11. General Remarks.—To receive the benefit of this Charity the object must be so far deprived of sight as not to have the use of it for necessary purposes.

HOME TEACHING SOCIETIES.

The number of Home Teaching Societies has so greatly increased since the first edition was published, that in the present edition we only give the names and addresses of the societies and secretaries. The object of them all is the same, viz., to teach the Blind at their homes to read in type for the Blind.

We are indebted to the report of the Home Teaching Society for the Blind, New Bridge Street, Blackfriars, London, for the full list we are enabled to give.

LONDON AND PROVINCIAL HOME TEACHING SOCIETIES FOR THE BLIND.

Place	When commenced	Name and Address of Secretary, Treasurer, or Superintendent
London	1855	G. MARTIN TAIT.
Aberdeen	1858	
Accrington	—	JAMES TOWNSON, Esq.
Ashton	1883	Rev. A. HALL.
Bangor	1882	Capt. VERNEY, Rhianva.
Bedford	1880	Miss MITCHELL.
Birkenhead	1874	Rev. CANON KNOX.
Birmingham	1858	
Blackburn	1881	Miss LUND.
Boston	1880	Miss JACKSON.
Bradford	1860	Misses GALE and HOLLOWAY.
Bradford (Wilts)	1879	Rev. H. LAMBERT.
Bristol	1857	
Burnley	1882	Mrs. RAWLINSON.
Cambridge	1876	Mrs. STEELE.
Cardiff	1865	J. HALL, Esq., Cornwall Villa.
Carlisle	1856	Miss H. JOHNSON, 6 Fisher Street.
Cheltenham	1858	Colonel IMPEY, The Park.
Chester	1875	Mrs. HOWSON, Deanery.
Colchester	1876	Mrs. H. CHURCH.
Cork	1861	
Cornwall	1857	C. TWEEDY, Esq., Redruth.
Coventry	1878	Alderman BANKS.
Derby	1862	T. HEATH, Esq.
Doncaster	1864	Mrs. R. C. CLARKE.
Droitwich	1880	Miss RICKETS.
Dublin	1858	Miss MARY PETTIGREW.
Dundee	1862	J. HUNTER, Esq.
Edinburgh	1856	J. BURN MURDOCK, Esq.
Folkestone and Dover	—	Miss TAYLOR.
Forfar & County of Dundee	1870	D. SLUTE, Esq.
Glasgow	1859	JAMES MILLER, Esq.
Gloucester	1880	Rev. M. TROTTER.
Great Grimsby	1880	Rev. J. YOUNG.
Greenock	1859	

INSTITUTIONS AND CHARITIES FOR THE BLIND.

LONDON & PROVINCIAL HOME TEACHING SOCIETIES FOR THE BLIND.

Place	When commenced	Name and Address of Secretary, Treasurer, or Superintendent
Guildford	1877	Mrs. PAYNTER.
Halifax	1856	Mrs. HARGREAVES.
Hereford	1880	Mrs. EDWARDS.
Huddersfield	1856	Miss WOOD.
Hull	1864	T. PRIESTMAN, Esq.
Inverness	—	
Ipswich	1869	H. C. CHEVALLIER, Esq.
Kidderminster	1880	Mrs. MAYNE.
Leeds	1858	Miss GROVER.
Leicester	1867	S. HARRIS, Esq.
Lincoln	1880	Rev. the SUB-DEAN.
Liverpool	1857	Miss WAINWRIGHT, Liverpool.
Luton	1880	Miss BETHAM.
Macclesfield	1875	Mrs. HENDERSON.
Manchester	1861	Rev. T. H. GILL, 5 Hyde Road.
Montrose	1867	
Newcastle-on-Tyne	1862	
Newport	1873	
Newport (Mon.)	1865	Rev. T. LISTER, Stow Hill.
Northampton	1879	The RURAL DEAN.
North Devon	1870	J. PARTRIDGE, Esq., Barnstaple.
Northumberland & Durham	1873	Rev. J. ORMSBY, Rainton.
Oldham	1878	Rev. A. J. J. CACHEMAILLE, M.A.
Oxford	1877	F. J. SPURLING, Esq., M.A.
Paisley	1859	
Perth	1859	Rev. W. D. KNOWLES, B.A.
Preston	—	
Richmond (Surrey)	1856	Miss PATON, Clapham.
Rochdale	1878	Mr. CALMAN.
Salisbury	1879	Miss JAGOB and Miss SNOW.
Sheffield	1858	Miss HARRISON.
Shrewsbury	1861	Mrs. WIGHTMAN, St. Alkmund.
Southampton	1879	Miss BROWN and Miss LAVER.
Southsea	1864	
Stirling	—	
Stoke *	1874	Rev. Sir LOVELACE STAMER, Bart.
Sunderland	1873	Rev. W. R. BURNET, St. Thomas.
Swansea	1865	
Trowbridge	1856	Mrs. WILKINS.
Wakefield	1873	Miss FENNEL, Westgate.
Wolverhampton	1874	Mrs. WHITEHOUSE.
Worcester	1869	Miss E. P. BREAY.
Worcestershire	—	Rev. S. S. FORSTER.
Yarmouth	1876	Mrs. GRIFFITHS.

* Operations at present suspended.

London School-Board Classes for the Blind.

The places and times are liable to change.

North End, West Brompton, S.W., Thursday afternoon.
Bowling-green Lane, Farringdon Road, Clerkenwell, E.C., every morning.
High Street, Shadwell, E., every afternoon.
Park Wall, Chelsea, S.W., Monday, Wednesday, and Friday morning.
Princes Street, Bedford Row, W.C., Thursday morning.
Church Street, Kennington, S.E., Monday, Tuesday, and Friday afternoon.
Portobello Road, Notting Hill, W., Tuesday and Thursday morning, Wednesday afternoon.
Waterloo Street, Hammersmith, W., Monday morning.
Stephen Street, Lisson Grove, N.W., Friday afternoon.
Pulteney Schools, Soho, W., Tuesday afternoon.
Haverstock Hill, N.W., Thursday afternoon.
Caledonian Road, Islington, N., Wednesday morning.
British Street, Millwall, E., Friday afternoon.
Anglers' Gardens, Popham Road, Islington, N., Monday afternoon.
Maidstone Street, Haggerstone, E., Tuesday morning.
South Grove, Mile End, E., Wednesday morning.
Scrutton Street, Shoreditch, E., Wednesday afternoon.
Cranbrook Road, Old Ford, E., Tuesday afternoon and Thursday morning.
Ricardo Street, Poplar, E., Monday afternoon.
Essex Street, Stepney, E., Thursday afternoon.
Burrage Grove, Plumstead, Wednesday afternoon.
Mina Road, Walworth, S.E., Tuesday morning.
Keeton's Road, Bermondsey, S.E., Wednesday morning.
Winchester Street, King's Cross, N., Friday afternoon.
Poole's Park, Upper Holloway, N., Monday morning.
Mantua Street, York Road, Battersea, S W., Friday afternoon.
Westmoreland Road, Walworth, S.E., Tuesday morning, Thursday afternoon.
Saxon Street, Bermondsey, S.E., Thursday morning.
All Saints, Lyham Road, Brixton, S.W., Tuesday afternoon.

List of Books, &c., on the Subject of the Blind. Known to the Authors.

Date of Publication.

1747 Life of Nicholas Sanderson, Professor at Cambridge, by John Inchliff.—Publisher, ' ——,' Dublin.

1749 Lettre sur les Aveugles, par M. Diderot, à Londres.

1773 An Essay on Blindness, translated from the French of M. Diderot —Publisher, Dymott, London.

1775 The Defeats of Police, &c., with Observations on the Rev. Mr. Hetherington's Charity for the Blind, by Jonas Hanway, Esq.—Publisher, J. Dodsley, Pall Mall, London.

1786 Essai sur l'Education des Aveugles, par M. Haüy, Rue Notre-Dame-des-Victoires.—Imprimé, par M. Clousier, Paris.

1793 The Education of the Blind, by M. Haüy, Paris, 1786, translated into English by Rev. Dr. Blacklock, and printed by A. Chapman and Co., Edinburgh, and T. Cadell, London.

1795 Life of John Metcalf, of Knaresborough.—Publishers, E. and R. Peck, York.

1813 Life of James Downing (blind).—Publisher, Haddon, London.

1816 Hints respecting the Employment of the Blind, by John Coakley Lettsom, M.D. and LL.D., &c., vol. ii., pp. 117-140.—Publishers, Nichols, Son, and Bentley, Red Lion Court Passage, Fleet Street, London.

1817 Essai sur l'Instruction des Aveugles, par le Docteur Guillié.—Imprimé par les Aveugles, Paris.

1819 An Essay on the Blind, translated from the French of Dr. Guillié.—Publisher, Phillips, London.

1825 Gentleman's Magazine, vol. xcv., p. 525.

1828 The Oxford Encyclopædia, vol. i., 'Blindness.'—Publisher, Thomas Kelley, 17 Paternoster Row, London.

1828 Gentleman's Magazine, vol. xcviii., p. 71 and p. 628.

1829 Life of John Metcalf (blind), by ——.—Publisher, Langdale, Knaresborough.

BOOKS.—*Continued.*

1833 The North American Review, vol. xxxvii., No. lxxx., pp. 20-58.—Publisher, Charles Bowen, 141 Washington Street, Boston.

1834 The Gospel by St. John for the Blind, with some Historical Notices regarding the origin and establishment of a tangible literature for their use, by James Gall.—Publishers, James Gall, 24 Niddry Street, Edinburgh; Hamilton, Adams, and Co., London; William Curry, jun., and Co., Dublin.

1834 Account of the Glasgow Asylum for the Blind, by James Gall.

1834 Literature for the Blind, by James Gall.—Publisher, Gall, Edinburgh.

1837 The Education of the Blind, by James Gall.—Publisher, Gall, Edinburgh.

1837 Observations on the Employment, &c., of the Blind, by Thomas Anderson.—Publishers, Simpkin and Marshall, London.

1837 Report on the Alphabets for the Blind, in the Transactions of the Royal Scotch Society of Arts, by the Rev. W. Taylor, F.R.S.

1837 Le Sourd-muet et l'Aveugle, par l'Abbé C. Carton.—Imprimerie de Vandecasteele, Werbrouck, Bruges.

1837 Essai sur l'Etat Physique, Moral et Intellectuel des Aveugles-nés, par P. A. Dufau.—A l'Imprimerie Royale, Paris.

1838 Les Etablissements pour les Aveugles en Angleterre, par l'Abbé C. Carton.—Imprimerie de Vandecasteele, Werbrouck, Bruges.

1838 Biography of the Blind, by James Wilson (blind).—Publisher, Showell, Birmingham.

1839 Blindness, by Andrew Park.—Publishers, Smith and Elder, London.

1842 An Account of the Institution for the Blind at Boston, United States, in 'American Notes,' vol. i., page 74, by Charles Dickens.—Publishers, Chapman and Hall, London.

1843 The Mental State of the Blind, Deaf, and Dumb, by R. Fowler, M.D.—Publisher, Brodie, Salisbury.

1843 The Punctiuncula Stenographic System of Embossing, by G. A. Hughes (blind).—Publisher, Hughes, London.

1844 Report of the British Association, p. 99.

BOOKS.—*Continued.*

1845 The Lost Senses (Blindness), by John Kitto, D.D.—Publisher, Knight, London.

1846 Education and Employment at the Asylum for Blind at Glasgow, by Mr. Alston.

1852 Report of the Jurors of the Great Exhibition of 1851, page 413, 'Printing for the Blind.'— Publisher, Clowes, London.

1852 An account of the School for the Blind at Paris, in 'Faggot of French Sticks,' vol. i., page 430, by Sir F. Head, Bart. —Publisher, Murray, London.

1853 Tangible Typography, by E. C. Johnson.— Publisher, Whitaker, London.

1853 A Lecture on the Education of the Blind in the Transactions of the Royal Institution of Great Britain, by the Rev. W. Taylor.—Publishers, Simpkin and Marshall, London.

1854 An Article in the Edinburgh Review, No. 201, page 61.— Publishers, Longmans, London.

1855 The Musical Instruction of the Blind in France, Spain, and America, by E. C. Johnson.— Publisher, Mitchell, London.

1855 'The Blind,' in 'Biographical and Critical Essays,' page 31, by W. H. Prescott (blind).—Publisher, Routledge, London.

1856 Life of James Wilson (blind), with an Essay, by John Bird, M.R.C.S. (blind).—Publishers, Ward and Lock, London.

1857 The Land of Silence, and The Land of Darkness, by the Rev. B. G. Johns.—Publishers, Longmans, London.

1857 'Songs in the Night:' a Lecture on the Triumphs of Genius over Blindness, page 59, in 'The Rifle, Axe, and Saddlebags,' by W. H. Milburn (blind). — Publisher, Sampson Low, London.

1859 The Sense Denied and Lost, by Thomas Bull, M.D. (blind.) —Publisher, Longman, London.

1859 The Education of the Blind, and on the Establishment of a College for those in the opulent classes : a paper read before the Social Science Society at Liverpool, September, 1858, by the Rev. W. Taylor, F.R.S.—Publisher, J. E. Taylor, London.

1859 The Blind: an article in the English Cyclopædia, reprinted, by Charles Baker.—Publisher, Knight, London.

Books.—*Continued.*

1859 On the Relation of the Blind to the World around them, translated from J. W. Klein's 'Die Anstalten für Blinde in Wien,' by the Rev. W. Taylor, F.R.S.—Publisher, J. E. Taylor, London.

1859 A short Sketch of the Life of J. W. Klein, Founder of the Institution for the Blind in Vienna, translated by Rev. W. Taylor, F.R.S.—Publisher, J. E. Taylor, London.

1859 Darkness and Light, by Mrs. W. Fison.—Publishers, Wertheim and Co., London.

1860 The Blind of London, by E. C. Johnson.—Publisher, Mitchell, London.

1860 The Irish Pauper Blind, by E. C. Johnson.—Publisher, Mallett, London.

1860 The Blind, by A. Mitchell (blind).—Publisher, Moorish, London.

1861 The Management and Education of Blind Children of J. G. Knie (Breslau), translated by Rev. W. Taylor.—Publishers, Simpkin and Marshall, London.

1861 Hammock's Census of the Blind, and the Deaf and Dumb, price 18s.

1862 L'Instituteur des Aveugles, par J. Guadet, Paris.

1862 The present Condition and future Improvement of the Blind, by J. W. Clare, Civil Engineer (blind).—Publisher, ——, London.

1862 What is doing for the Blind, by James Gray (blind).—Publishers, Gall and Inglis, Edinburgh.

1862 Social Pathology. The Blind, and the Deaf and Dumb, by John Bird, M.R.C.S. (blind.)—Publishers, Ward and Lock, London.

1862 On the Number and Condition of the Blind in Ireland. A paper read before the Congrès International de Bienfaisance, by W. R. Wilde, M.D.

1863 Report on Printing for the Blind in the Transactions of the British Association for the Advancement of Science, by the Rev. W. Taylor.—Publishers, Simpkin and Marshall, London.

1863 The Census of England and Wales for the year 1861. General Report, presented to Parliament, vol. iii., pages 42, 164, &c. Printers, Eyre and Spottiswoode.

Books.—*Continued.*

1863 The Deaf, Dumb, and Blind: a letter to Rev. R. Maguire, M.A., by John Bird, M.R.C.S. (blind). — Publishers, Ward and Lock, London.

1863 An Article in the Social Science Report for May.

1864 The Education of the Blind, and the Deaf and Dumb. A Lecture by Alfred Payne.—Publisher, Tweedie, London.

1864 Facts and Figures, by E. Moore.— Publisher, Aylott, London.

1864 Charity misapplied, by Mrs. Hippolyte van Landeghem (blind).—Publisher, Bessy, Stockwell.

1865 Exile and Home, by Mrs. Hippolyte van Landeghem (blind).—Publisher, Clowes, London.

1865 An Article in the Quarterly Review, No. 236, page 430.— Publisher, Murray, London.

1866 A Lecture on the best mode of Relieving the Blind, by T. J. Dunning.—Publisher, Taylor, London.

1867 Blind People, their Works and Ways, by the Rev. B. G. Johns, M.A.—Publisher, Murray, London.

1867 A few remarks on the Blind Industrial Exhibition, 1867, by E. Moore.—Publisher, Moore, London.

1867 The College at Worcester for the Blind Sons of Gentlemen. Reprinted by request from the *Worcester Herald* of December 7th, 1867.

1867 An Account of the Blind School at Illzach, near Mülhausen, in the 'Romance of Charity,' page 395, by John de Liefde.—Publisher, Strahan, London.

1868 Paris Exhibition, 1867. Apparatus, &c., for the Blind. Report presented to Parliament by E. C. Johnson.— Publishers, Eyre and Spottiswoode, London.

1868 A Blind Inventor. The Life of Dr. Gale, M.A., F.G.S., F.C.S., inventor of the non-explosive gunpowder processes, by John Plummer.—Publisher, Tweedie, London.

1868 Education of the Blind. A Paper read at the Meeting of the Association for Promoting Social Science, at Birmingham, October, 1868, by Rev. R. H. Blair, M.A., London.

1870 A Plea for the Blind, and a reprint of Mr. Blackstock's Evidence before the Parliamentary Committee of Inquiry into the working of the Poor Law Board of Scotland. Publisher, Macrone, Glasgow.

Books.—*Continued.*

1870 The Education and Literature of the Blind. Report of a Meeting at Worcester, reprinted from the *Worcester Herald*, December, 1869. London.

1871 The Education and Employment of the Blind; what it has been, is, and ought to be, by T. R. Armitage, M.D.—Publisher, Hardwicke, London.

1871 Piano-tuning as an Employment for the Blind. A Paper in the Journal of the Society of Arts, January 6, 1871, by T. R. Armitage, M.D.

1871 Proceedings of the Second Convention of American Instructors of the Blind, held at Indiana Institute, August, 1871. Printed at the Indianapolis Printing and Publishing House.

1871 London International Exhibition, 1871. Official Report on the methods of Teaching the Blind, and the Deaf and Dumb, by Edmund C. Johnson.

1872 Blindness and the Blind, by W. Hanks Levy, F.R.G.S. (blind).—Publishers, Chapman and Hall, 193 Piccadilly, London.

1873 Census of England and Wales (1871), General Report, vol. iv., page 54.—Printers, Eyre and Spottiswoode, London.

1873 The New York System of Tangible Musical Notation and Point Writing and Printing for the Blind.—Publishers, Bradstreet Press, 279 Broadway, New York.

1873 Light for the Blind, by William Moon, LL.D., F.R.G.S. (blind).—Publishers, Longman and Co., London.

1873 The Friend of the Blind: suggestions by the South London Mission for the Blind, 38 Kennington Road, Lambeth.—Printer, W. Wayne, 22 Lower Kennington Lane.

1875 The Training of the Blind: extracts from the Report of the First European Congress of Teachers of the Blind held at Vienna, August, 1873; translated by Major-General Bainbrigge, R.E.—Publishers, Charity Organisation Society, 15 Buckingham Street, Adelphi, London.

1875 A New Era in the Education of Blind Children, by Alexander Barnhill.—Publishers, Houlston and Sons, London; Charles Glass and Co., 85 Maxwell Street, Glasgow.

BOOKS.—*Continued.*

1875 The Future of the Blind, by S. S. Foster, M.A.—Publishers, Simpkin, Marshall, and Co., London.

1875 The Consequences and Ameliorations of Blindness, by William Moon, LL.D. (blind).—Publishers, Longmans and Co., Paternoster Row, London.

1876 The Training of the Blind: a Report of a Special Committee of the Charity Organisation Society, 15 Buckingham Street, Adelphi, London.—Publishers, Longmans, Green, and Co., London.

1876 The Education of the Blind, by Robert Hugh Blair, M.A., F.R.A.S., &c.—Publishers, Simpkin, Marshall, and Co., London.

1876 The School Board for London Report of Conference on the Instruction of Blind Children, and conclusions arrived at, by the School Management Committee of the Board.

1876 Annuities to the Blind, by Edmund C. Johnson.—Publisher, Henry Roberts, 2 Arabella Street, Pimlico.

1877 Hints to Blind Home Students, by Robert Hugh Blair, M.A , F.R.A.S.—Publishers, Holl and Darke, Worcester.

1878 The Condition of the Blind of Great Britain and Ireland, by T. R. Armitage, M.D.—Publishers, Gilbert and Rivington, London.

1879 A Statement on the General Question of the Blind and the best mode of improving their Condition, prepared by a Member of the Council of the Charity Organisation Society (London) for the consideration of those interested in the Blind.—Publishers, Spottiswoode and Co., New Street Square, London.

1879 Two Reports made by F. J. Munby, Hon. Sec. of the School for the Blind at York, and A. Buckle, superintendent of that School:—

    1. On the Articles exhibited by Blind Institutions at the Exposition Universelle, Paris, 1878.

    2. The National Institution for the Young Blind in Paris.

Publishers, W. Sotheran and Co., Petergate, York.

1879 The Taylor Arithmetic, by W. H. Taylor (blind), Stockton-on-Tees.—College for the Blind, Worcester.

Books.—*Continued.*

1879 Congrès Universel pour l'Amélioration du sort des aveugles et des sourds-muets, tenu à Paris du 23 au 30 Septembre. Imprimerie Nationale, Paris.

1879 Report made to the Managing Committee of the School for the Blind at York on the International Congress for the Amelioration of the Condition of the Blind held in Paris, September, 1878, by A. Buckle, B.A.—Publishers, Coultas and Volans, King Street, York.

1879 The Education of the Blind. Three papers read at the Paris Congress, 1878 :—
    1. By M. von Pablasek, of Vienna.
    2. By J. Moldenhawer, of Copenhagen.
    3. By A. Buckle, of York.
Publishers, W. Sotheran and Co., Petergate, York.

1879 What shall we do with our Blind Boys? by S. S. Foster, M.A.—Publishers, W. Kent and Co., London.

1879 The Present State of the Physique of the Blind, by Dr. Roth, 48 Wimpole Street, London.

1879 Social Notes, January 11, by W. ———.—Published, 16 Southampton Street, Strand, London.

1880 The Eleventh Report of the Charity Organisation Society, 15 Buckingham Street, Adelphi, London. Pages 19, 20, 31.

1880 The 'Gardner' Bequest for the Blind, by S. S. Foster, M.A.—Publisher, Alfred M. Bayliss, New Street, Worcester.

1880 High Court of Justice, Chancery Division, Henry Gardner, deceased (bequest for the Blind), affidavit of C. S. Loch, Esq.—Printer, T. Scott, Warwick Court, Holborn, London.

1881 England's Blind Sons and Daughters, by H. J. R. Marston, M.A. (blind).—Publishers, Andrews and Co., Durham.

1881 The Education of the Blind. The adaptation of Froebel's Kindergarten System for the Blind, by William Martin, Manager, Royal Blind Asylum and School, Edinburgh.

1883 The Census of England and Wales (1881). General Report, vol. iv., page 60, &c.—Printers, Eyre and Spottiswoode, London.

1883 Light on Dark Paths, by R. Meldrum.—Publishers, D. Wyllie and Son, Aberdeen.

1883 Yorkshire School for the Blind. Report of the Jubilee Celebration and of the Conference of Managers and Teachers and Friends of the Blind, held at York, July, 1883.—Printed at the *Daily Herald* Office, York.

BOOKS.—*Continued.*

1883 Industrial Employment of the Blind working in Institutions. A Paper read at the Jubilee Celebration of the Yorkshire School for the Blind, 1883, by William Martin, Manager of the Royal Blind Asylum and School, Edinburgh, and Honorary Member of the International Society for the Amelioration of the Condition of the Blind.—(Printed for private circulation.)

1883 The Prevention of Blindness. A Paper read at the Jubilee Celebration of the Yorkshire School for the Blind (1883), by Dr. M. Roth, of 48 Wimpole Street, London.—Printed at the *Daily Herald* Office, York.

1883 Report of the New York State Board of Charities on the Number and Condition of the Indigent Blind.

1884 Notes on the Report of the Jubilee Conference, held at York in July, 1883, to consider the Condition of the Blind, by X X.—Publishers, Kegan Paul, Trench, and Co., 1 Paternoster Square, London.

No date. The Claims of the Blind.—Publisher, J. Maxwell, Edinburgh.

  „   The Condition of the Blind.—Publisher, T. Campbell, Edinburgh.

  „   The Genius of the Blind.—Publisher, E. H. White, London.

  „   An Article, 'Blind,' in the Encyclopædia Britannica, by Blacklock.

  „   Major Beniowski's Phrenotypic Primer for the Blind.—Published by the author, 8 Bond Street, London.

  „   An Article, 'Printing for the Blind,' in 'Tomlinson's Cyclopædia of Useful Arts,' part 32.—Publisher, Virtue, London.

  „   An Article, 'Blind,' in Chambers' Encyclopædia, No. 62, p. 155.—Publishers, Chambers, Edinburgh.

  „   Anecdotes of the Deaf, Dumb, and Blind, in Chambers' 'Miscellany of Instructive Tracts,' No. 44.—Publishers, Chambers, Edinburgh.

  „   Authentic Anecdotes and Biographical Sketches of Remarkable Blind Persons, by Gavin Douglas.—Publisher, Smeeton, London.

Lehrbuch zum Unterrichte der Blinden. Klein.
Geschichte des Unterrichts der Blinden. Klein.
Anleitung für blinde Kinder, &c. Klein.

BOOKS.—*Continued.*

Jakob Braun. Klein.
Anstalten für Blinde. Klein.
Lieder für Blinde. Klein.
Beschreibung eines gelungenen Versuches blinder Kinder zur bürg. Brauchbarkeit zu bilden. Klein.
Nachrichten von einigen Blindgeborenen, &c. Rotermund.
An Regierungen, Elter, und Lehrer, &c. Daniel.
Ueber die Behandlung welcher blinde Kinder, &c. Jäger.
Blinden-Anstalt in Zürich. Oreill.
Ansichten über die Erziehung der Zöglinge einer Blinden-Anstalt, &c. Dolezálek.
Ueber die Erziehung und den Unterricht der Blinden, &c. Hienzsch.
Geschichte der K. S. Blinden-Anstalt zu Dresden. Georgi.
Kurzer Unterricht für Eltern und Lehrer der Blinden. Struve.
Belisar, oder über Blinde und Blinden-Anstalten. Zeune.
Gründliche Hülfe für Blinde, &c. Freudenberg.
Ueber mich selbst und meine Unglücksgefährten, die Blinden. Baczko.
Ideen über Musik. Prince George of Denmark.

Also the works of Knie, Müller, Niboyet, Hirzel, Nageli, Koch, Wolke, Altorfer, Neudegg, Lachmann, Braille.

Publishers of Books in Embossed Type.

Books, in raised Roman Letters, for the use of the Blind, are sold at the GLASGOW ASYLUM FOR THE BLIND, and may be had from the Institution through any bookseller in the United Kingdom.

The list contains the Bible, and some few religious and educational works.

A few books for the Blind, in Roman characters, are published at the SCHOOL FOR THE BLIND, St. George's Fields, London, S.E.

A few books for the Blind, in Roman characters, are published at the ASYLUM FOR THE BLIND, Park Street, Bristol.

Books, in Roman characters, are published by the SOCIETY FOR

BOOKS IN EMBOSSED TYPE.—*Continued.*
PROVIDING CHEAP LITERATURE FOR THE BLIND, 33 College Street, Worcester. Principally religious and educational works.

Works for the Blind in Moon's type, published by DR. MOON, 104 Queen's Road, Brighton.—Any person who may wish to have a particular chapter of the Bible, hymn, or other work stereotyped, can do so, on terms which can be ascertained by applying to Dr. Moon, a perfect copy of which will be presented to the donor on the completion of the work, but the plates will be retained as the property of the Charity.

The list contains the Bible, books for beginners and aged, Religious works, History, Poetry, Tales and Anecdotes, Remarkable Answers to Prayer, Memoirs, on Temperance, Educational, Scientific and General, Music, Maps, Astronomical Maps and apparatus for writing, also portions of Bible in thirty-two foreign languages.

Books, in Braille type, and Educational Appliances can be obtained from the BRITISH AND FOREIGN BLIND ASSOCIATION for Promoting the Education and Employment of the Blind, 33 Cambridge Square, Hyde Park, London, W.

The list of books in Braille Type contains the Bible, Religious works, Scientific works, History, Poetry, Fiction, Educational, with apparatus for writing, and a full catalogue of Music. A Magazine for the Blind, in Braille Type, is published every two months, as a means of information for the Blind on subjects in which they are specially interested.

Publications of the LONDON SOCIETY FOR TEACHING THE BLIND TO READ, in T. M. Lucas's embossed stenographic characters. Sold, bound in half-cloth, by the BRITISH AND FOREIGN BIBLE SOCIETY, Blackfriars; by Messrs. NISBET, Berners Street, W.; and at the school, Upper Avenue Road, Regent's Park, N.W.

The list contains works on Religion, Poetry, Education, Music, Anecdotes, and the whole Bible.

Works published by the SOCIETY FOR PROVIDING CHEAP LITERATURE FOR THE BLIND: offices, College Street, Worcester (Mr. J. J. W. Stoyle, Secretary).

The list contains books in large-sized type for hard hands, and in small type for educated persons, and works on Religion, Poetry, Education, Greek and Latin Classics, Anecdotes, Fiction, with apparatus for education.

The BRITISH AND FOREIGN BIBLE SOCIETY supplies Scriptures in embossed types, Moon and Braille. Many books in Roman type are published in America.

Various Systems of Embossed Type that are, or have been, in Use by the Blind.

Alston's. Invented by Dr. Fry, of London. Full Letter. Roman Capitals. Books published at Glasgow Asylum for the Blind.

Braille's. Full Letter, and with contractions. Dots. Books published at 33 Cambridge Square, London, W.

Frere's. Phonetic. Arbitrary. Books published at 27 Red Lion Square, London, W.C.

Gall's. Full Letter. Angular Roman. Books published by J. Gall, Niddry Street, Edinburgh.

Howe's. Full Letter. Angular Roman. Books published at Boston Institution for the Blind, United States.

Lucas's. Stenographic. Books published at St. John's Wood School for the Blind, London, N.W.

Mitford's. Full Letter. Roman Characters placed vertically. Books published at Mitford's, Cheltenham.

Moon's. Full Letter. Modified Roman and Arbitrary. Books published at Mr. Moon's, 104 Queen's Road, Brighton.

Worcester. Full Letter. Ordinary Roman characters. Books published by the Society for Providing Cheap Literature for the Blind, High Street, Worcester, and 33 Essex Street, Strand, London.

Stuttgardt. Full Letter. Roman capitals, formed of Dots.

List of Appliances that have become known to the Authors as having been made at various times for the Use of the Blind, but which they are not in a position to guarantee are now to be obtained.

A Portfolio for the Blind to write with a style, by G. Spencer (blind), Rugby.

A Machine for enabling the Blind to write in raised characters without types, by Mr. A. E. Hughes, 9 Mount Row, Westminster Road, London.

APPLIANCES.—*Continued.*

A Machine to write with a pen or pencil in skeleton Roman capitals, by Mr. A. E. Hughes, 9 Mount Row, Westminster Road, London.

A Machine to cast accounts, and make arithmetical calculations, by tangible characters, by Mr. A. E. Hughes, 9 Mount Row, Westminster Road, London.

A Machine to copy and compose music on paper, by Mr. A. E. Hughes, 9 Mount Row, Westminster Road, London.

Stenographical Treatise, by Mr. A. E. Hughes, 9 Mount Row, Westminster Road, London.

An improved Noctograph, for persons who have become blind after having learned to write, by Mr. Wedgwood, Lombard Street, London.

Ciphering Board for the Blind; to be had at the School for the Blind, Avenue Road, Regent's Park, London.

Maps for the Blind; to be had at the School for the Blind, Avenue Road, Regent's Park, London.

Geometrical Board for the Blind; to be had at the School for the Blind, Avenue Road, Regent's Park, London.

Music for the Blind; to be had at the School for the Blind, Avenue Road, Regent's Park, London.

Chess Board for the Blind; to be had at the School for the Blind, Avenue Road, Regent's Park, London.

Apparatus for enabling the Blind to emboss Lucas's characters; to be had at the School for the Blind, Avenue Road, Regent's Park, London.

Tangible Ink for the Blind, by Dr. Foulis; to be had at the School for the Blind, Edinburgh.

Manuscript music notation for the Blind, by Dr. Foulis; to be had at the School for the Blind, Edinburgh.

Typhlograph for the Blind, by Mr. James Gall, Myrtle Bank, Edinburgh.

Apparatus for writing by and to the Blind, by Mr. James Gall, Myrtle Bank, Edinburgh.

Writing Apparatus on Martuscelli's system (Naples).

Writing Apparatus for persons becoming blind at advanced age, by Captain L. Schuytkorver (blind), of the Royal Dutch Navy (retired).

Writing Apparatus, by Major J. P. Serraris, Bart. (blind).

APPLIANCES.—*Continued.*

Writing Apparatus, by C. Pooley, F.S.A., price 21s.

Writing Apparatus, by Dr. Thursfield; makers, Elliott Brothers, 449 Strand, London; price 42s.

Apparatus used by Blind Shoemakers, by Herr Moldenhawer, of Copenhagen.

Arithmetic for the Blind, by Mr. James Gall, Myrtle Bank, Edinburgh.

A Writing Machine for the Blind, producing the characters in black or in relief, by G. B. Marchesi, Lodi, Austria.

A Portable Writing Machine for the Blind, by the late W. Hughes, Blind Asylum, Manchester; to be had at Mr. G. A. Wyld's, 47 Everton Road, Manchester.

Instrument for Teaching the Blind to Write, by W. B. Tollutt, Folkestone.

Writing Apparatus for the Blind, by Pierre Foucault, 28 Rue de Charenton, aux Quinze-Vingts, Paris (blind).

An Instrument for Teaching the Blind to Draw and Write, by Robert Thompson, Columbus, Ohio, U.S.

Writing Machine for the Blind, by John Martin, Alfreton Road, Nottingham.

A System of Embossed Music for the Blind, by J. St. Clair, 13 South Frederick Street, Edinburgh.

Embossing Press for the Blind, by Mr. Harris, 3 Gratton Terrace, Cheltenham.

A Weather Guide.

Needles.

A Mariner's Compass, by Rev. W. Taylor and W. H. Levy.

Texin's Patent Mechanical Needle Threader.

A Pen Guide to enable the Blind to write with ink, by W. H. Levy (blind), 127 Euston Road, London.

Embossed writing copies, by W. H. Levy, 127 Euston Road, London.

A Card to enable the Blind to write with a pencil, by W. H. Levy, 127 Euston Road, London.

Apparatus to enable the Blind to write so that their letters may be read by either the blind or sighted, by W. H. Levy, 127 Euston Road, London.

thmetical Apparatus, by W. H. Levy, 127 Euston Road, London.

APPLIANCES.—*Continued.*

- A Pocket Yard Measure, by W. H. Levy, 127 Euston Road, London.
- Writing Desk for the Blind, by J. G. Calkin, 12 Clayton Street, Kennington, S.E.
- Frame and letters for teaching the alphabet, by M. von Pablasek, Imperial Blind Institution, Vienna.
- Embossing Press on Braille's system, by M. von Pablasek, Imperial Blind Institution, Vienna.
- Writing Frames for Braille's system, T. R. Armitage, M.D., 33 Cambridge Square, London.
- Writing Machine, Mr. Hebold, Blind School, Barley, Prussia.
- A Handguide for writing with a pencil in the ordinary caligraphy of the seeing, by Mr. C. E. Guldberg, Institution for the Blind, Copenhagen.
- Embossing Frame and Roller for enabling the Blind to emboss. S. H. Murley, Esq., Cheltenham.
- A Mechanical Contrivance for enabling the Blind to Print, by Mr. D. Nekols, Manchester.
- Tangible Arithmetic Frame; Dissected Maps. The Society for Providing Cheap Literature for the Blind, Worcester.
- Type for puncturing paper, Mr. James Galpin, 127 Caledonian Road, London.
- Euclid for the Blind, by Mr. Clarke, Type-founder, Canonbury, London.
- Davy's Skep-gage, Bradford Institution for the Blind, price 3*l.* 4*s.*
- L'Electro-Lecteur ou Machine à lire, à l'Usage des Aveugles, M. Ernest Recordon, 10 Rue Nicolas Flamel, Paris, 1874.
- Clip-folios for binding embossed writing.
- Clip-folios small size.
- Arithmetic Boards, by the late Rev. W. Taylor; Pegs for Arithmetic Boards; Cards for pencil writing; embossing papers; from London Society for Teaching Blind to Read, 33 Cambridge Square, London, W.
- Raised Maps, by W. Martin and Co., 67 West Nile Street, Glasgow.
- Maps in Relief, by Home and Colonial School Society, 350 Gray's Inn Road, London.

Institutions for the Blind in Foreign Countries, so far as known to the Authors.

Place	When Founded	Place	When Founded
AMERICA.		**AUSTRALIA.**	
Boston	1831	Sidney	1869
New York	1832	Melbourne	1881
Philadelphia	1833	**BELGIUM.**	
Columbus	1837		
Staunton	1838	Brussels	1833
Louisville [1]	1842	Bruges	—
Nashville	1844	Antwerp	—
Batavia	1845	Gand	—
Indianapolis	1846	Liège	—
Jackson	1848	Mons	—
Jacksonville	1848	Namur	—
Raleigh	1848		
Jamesville	1849	**BOHEMIA.**	
Cedar Springs	1849	Prague	1807
St. Louis	1851	**CHINA.**	
Macon	1852	Shanghai	—
Iowa City	1853	Ningpo	—
Bâton Rouge	1853	**DENMARK.**	
Baltimore	1854	Copenhagen	1811
Flint	1854	Do. Workshops	1862
Washington	1854	**FRANCE.**	
Austin	1856		
Little Rock	1857	Paris School	1784
Alabama	1857	Do. Asylum	1791
San Francisco	1859	Quinze-Vingts	—
Fariboult	1862	Do. Workshops	1883
Wyandotte	1867	Lisle	—
		Lyons	—
AMERICA (BRITISH).		Marseilles	—
Montreal	—	Montpellier	—
Toronto	—	Nancy	—
Halifax	—	Soissons	—
AUSTRIA.		Poitiers	—
Vienna	1804	**GERMANY.**	
Do. Asylum	1825	Berlin	1806
Lintz	1824	Dresden	1809
Brünn (Moravia)	—	Königsberg	1818

[1] At Louisville, Kentucky, there is a National Printing Association for Printing books in embossed type.

INSTITUTIONS AND CHARITIES FOR THE BLIND.

INSTITUTIONS FOR BLIND IN FOREIGN COUNTRIES.—*Cont.*

Place	When Founded
GERMANY.—*Continued.*	
Breslau...	1819
Ymund...	1823
Munich	1825
Weimar	1825
Bruchsal	1826
Friesenburg	1828
Brunswick	1829
Hamburg	1830
Halle	1832
Mannheim	1846
Stettin	1851
Magdeburg	1853
Posen	1853
Wolstein	1853
Würzburg	1853
Mecklenburg-Schwerin	1856
Illzach (Mulhausen) ...	1856
Wiesbaden	1862
Düren (Cologne) ...	—
Ellwanger	—
Frankfort	—
Freiberg	—
Freidberg-Hesse ...	—
Gottenbourg	—
Hanover	—
Hubertusberg	—
Kiel	—
Barley	—
Leipzig	—
Metz	—
Nuremberg	—
Soest	—
Stuttgart	—
HOLLAND.	
Amsterdam	1803
Do. Workshops ...	1848
Gromugen.	

Place	When Founded
HOLLAND.—*Continued.*	
Rotterdam	1858
Utrecht	—
The Hague	—
HUNGARY.	
Pesth	1825
INDIA.	
Allahabad	—
ITALY.	
Naples...	1818
Milan	—
NORWAY.	
Christiania	—
RUSSIA.	
St. Petersburg ...	1806
Warsaw (Poland) ...	1825
Helsingfors (Finland)...	—
Gatchina (St. Petersburg)	—
Riga	—
SPAIN.	
Grenada	1823
Do. Plaza Santa Anna	1834
Madrid	1841
Barcelona	1850
SWEDEN.	
Stockholm	1806
SWITZERLAND.	
Zurich	1809
Berne	—
Schaffhausen	—
Freiberg	—
Lausanne	—
SYRIA.	
Beyrout	—

The following Articles made by the Blind were exhibited at the International Exhibition at South Kensington, 1871.

Basket-Work.—Bath, Birmingham, Leicester, London (St. George's Fields), London (St. John's Wood), and York Institutions.

Basket.—Lausanne Institution.

Bead-Work Articles.—London (St. John's Wood) Institution.

Beehive.—Cheltenham Institution.

Beehive.—Delamere, Cheshire.

Bottle Envelopes.—Norwich Institution.

Bracelets made of Plaited Hair.—London (St. George's Fields), and York Institutions.

Box for Matches.—London.

Brushes and Brooms.—Birmingham, Leicester, London (Alexandra), London (St. George's Fields), and London (St. John's Wood) Institutions.

Carpet.—Aberdeen Institution.

Chair, made of Osiers.—London (St. John's Wood) Institution.

Chair-Seats in Cane.—Birmingham and Leicester Institutions.

Chair-Seats in Willow and Rushes.—Leicester Institution.

Carpet Beater, made of Cane.—Illzach, Mulhausen, Institution.

Clothes Line.—Aberdeen Institution.

Cup and Ball turned in a Lathe.—Paris Institution.

Dolls' Clothing.—London (Alexandra), London (St. George's Fields), and York Institutions.

Hassocks, made of Straw.—Cheltenham and Plymouth Institutions.

Hassocks, made of Rush Matting.—Leicester Institution.

Hassocks, made of Braid and American Leather.—Worcester Institution.

Hearth-rugs, made of Wool.—Birmingham and London (St. George's Fields) Institutions.

Hearth rugs, made of Listing.—Sheffield Institution.

American-Leather Work Articles.—Worcester Institution.

Mats of various kinds.—Birmingham, London (St. George's), and York Institutions.

Mat, made of Straw.—Illzach, Mulhausen, Institution.

Mat, made of Rushes.—Reading.

ARTICLES MADE BY THE BLIND.—*Continued.*

Mattress and Bedding.—Edinburgh Institution.
Matting, made of Jute.—Edinburgh Institution.
Matting, made of Manilla Hemp.—Aberdeen Institution.
Matting, made of Half-tarred Twine.—Liverpool (Hardman Street) Institution.
Mittens.—Illzach, Mulhausen, Institution.
Mops.—London (Euston Road) and Nottingham Institutions.
Needlework.—Illzach, Mulhausen, Institution.
Neck-tie, Woollen.—Illzach, Mulhausen, Institution.
Net, made of String (for Garden).—Brighton Institution.
Net, made of String (for Game Bag).—Aberdeen Institution.
Pincushion, made of Plaited Straw.—Worcester Institution.
Pincushion, made of Wood, turned in a lathe, with screw to fasten it to a Table.—Lausanne Institution.
Purse, knitted with Beads.—Paris Institution.
Purse, knitted with Beads.—Newcastle Institution.
Riddles.—Glasgow Institution.
Rope.—Aberdeen Institution.
Rope, made of Plaited Hemp.—Illzach, Mulhausen, Institution.
Sack.—London (Spitalfields) Institution.
Sackcloth.—Glasgow Institution.
Shawl, knitted, of Pyrenean Wool.—Bradford Institution.
Ship's Fender.—Liverpool (Cornwallis Street) Institution.
Shoes, made of Listing.—Lausanne Institution.
Shoes, made of Listing.—Illzach, Mulhausen, Institution.
Skipping Rope.—Illzach, Mulhausen, Institution.
Socks, knitted.—Southsea Institution.
Straw Plaited Articles.—Worcester Institution.
Tray, made of Wood.—London.
Twine, of various kinds.—Glasgow Institution.
Veil, for an Infant.—Southsea Institution.
Watch-guard, made of Plaited Hair.—London (St. George's Fields) and York Institutions.
Watch-guard, made of Plaited Braid.—Paris Institution.
Window-blind Cord.—Liverpool (Hardman Street) Institution.
Window-sash Line.—Liverpool (Hardman Street) Institution.
Wooden Articles turned in a Lathe.—Lausanne and Paris Institutions.

Acts of Parliament relating to the Blind generally.

The Poor Law Amendment Act of 3rd and 4th William IV., cap. 76, sec. 56.

The 25th and 26th Victoria, cap. 43, sec. 6, 7, and 10.

The 25th and 26th Victoria, cap. 43.

The 31st and 32nd Victoria, cap. 122, sec. 13 and 42.

Relating to Metropolis only.—The 30th and 31st Victoria, cap. 106, sec. 21; and the 30th and 31st Victoria, cap. 6, sec. 5.

www.ingramcontent.com/pod-product-compliance
Lightning Source LLC
Chambersburg PA
CBHW022135160426
43197CB00009B/1299